Understanding The Geography of the Bible

An Introductory Atlas

Menashe Har-El

Edited and expanded by

Paul H. Wright

cartaJerusalem

CONTENTS

List of Maps

Carta Jerusalem, Ltd.
18 Ha'uman Street, P.O.B. 2500, Jerusalem 9102401, Israel
Website: www.carta-jerusalem.com
E-mail: carta@carta.co.il

Cartography: Carta, Jerusalem

Photographs by Paul H. Wright
pp. 4, 6, 7, 10, 11, 13, 15, 16, 18, 19, 21–25, 26 (top), 30–32, 34 (top), 36 (top), 39, 40
Photograph on p. 3 by Mike Horton
Photograph on p. 28 (bottom) by NASA
All others from the archives of Carta, Jerusalem

ISBN: 978-965-220-863-7

Printed in the United States of America

Introduction

The marl caves of Qumran where the Dead Sea Scrolls were discovered, near the northwestern shore of the Dead Sea.

The majority of the biblical story took place in a very small yet interesting land nestled along the southeastern shore of the Mediterranean Sea, the land of Israel. To provide the proper geographical context of the biblical story, however, it is necessary to cast a wider net, one that encompasses Israel's neighbors near and far. While at its maximum the world of the Bible stretched from Susa in Persia (Esther 1:2) to possibly Spain (Romans 15:28), for practical purposes our sweep can be limited to two regions that intersect in Israel: to the south and east, the lands surrounding the Fertile Crescent (often called the ancient Near East) and to the north and west, the Mediterranean Basin as far as southern Italy. In a sense, a line dividing east from west is artificial, and the lands where the two meet (including Anatolia, Egypt's Nile Delta and the entire eastern seaboard of the Mediterranean) properly have characteristics of both. Yet it is sometimes helpful to make certain important generalizations up front, such as that the hill country of Israel tended to be oriented to the east, while the coastal plain more often than not faced the sea. This state of being in between the geographical and cultural forces of the ancient world has given variety, richness and depth to the biblical story.

CLIMATE

Introduction

It is often wondered if the climate of the Middle East today is the same as it was during the biblical period. While local fluctuations in climate—i.e., in temperature and aridity—can be traced over a period of years, decades or even centuries, a fair analysis of the data (including rock weathering, the presence of plant and animal species over time and historic patterns of human settlement) suggests that the overall climate of the Middle East has been essentially stable for at least the last five thousand years. In addition, biblical statements about climate (e.g. Deut 32:2; Job 38:22–30, 34–38; Ps 65:12–13; Prov 25:14; Jer 4:11; Mk 4:37) ring as real today as they did when they were first written. For this reason, it should be assumed that the following look at climate, although based on data of the modern Middle East, is applicable to that of the biblical world as well.

Several elements affect climate in the Middle East. Of these, the most important is *location*. Most of the countries of the Middle East lie between 15° and 40° north latitude, near the Tropic of Cancer (23.5° north of the equator). As a result, the climate throughout the region is largely subtropical. Within this subtropical zone lie some of the warmest and driest regions in the world, where long summers, subject to a sustained high barometric pressure, are characterized by high temperatures and no precipitation. The heat of the summer is intensified by the strong rays of the sun that enter the earth's atmosphere at an angle perpendicular to the Tropic of Cancer.

In winter, the sun moves southward to the Tropic of Capricorn (23.5° S), and westerly winds blow toward the Middle East over the Mediterranean Sea. For most of the winter the northern part of the Mediterranean is subject to a low barometric pressure characterized by high precipitation and cool temperatures. The winter's often heavy rains are born in the buoyant, humid air of the Atlantic Ocean and the Mediterranean Sea, air that rises, cools, condenses, and releases precipitation. The season's cool temperatures are a result of the horizontal angle of the sun's rays in and around the Tropic of Cancer.

Topography is the second element that affects climate. Plains and valleys are generally warmer and dryer in all seasons than are hilly or mountainous regions, which are generally cooler and wetter. For instance, the amount of precipitation that falls in coastal regions, in interior cold mountain recesses or in the warm heartlands will vary greatly. As a specific example, extreme temperature differences exist between the valleys and basins of the central Persian Plateau, which suffer from unbearable heat reaching 130° F (54° C) in the summer, and the peaks of the snow-covered mountains on its perimeter.

The third factor that affects climate is *proximity to large bodies of water*. Regions situated near oceans or seas will

The high, sandy desert of the central Sinai Peninsula offers harsh living conditions dictating the lifestyle of the Bedouin.

MEAN ANNUAL PRECIPITATION OF THE MIDDLE EAST

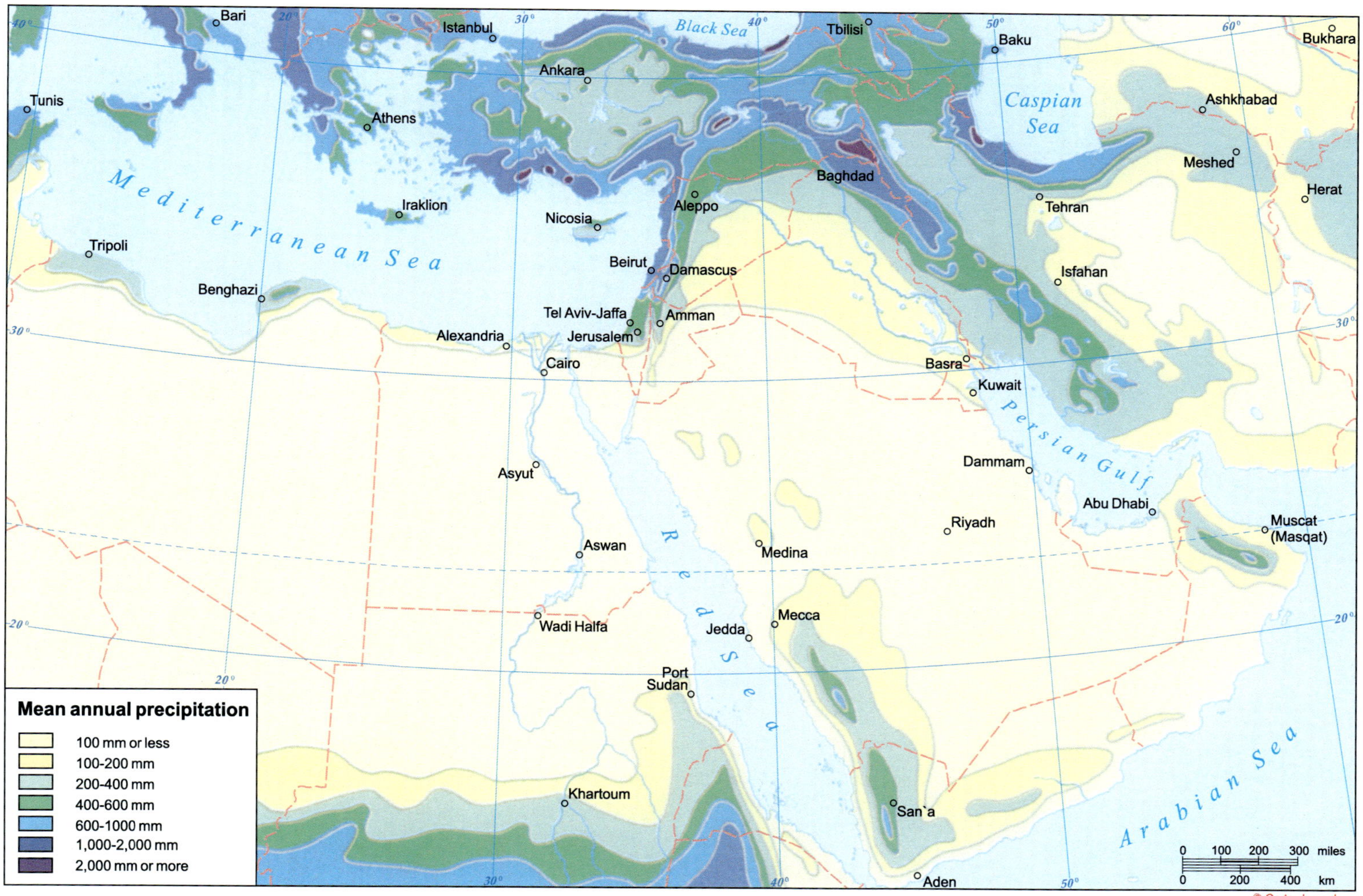

MEAN TEMPERATURES OF JANUARY

MEAN TEMPERATURES OF JULY

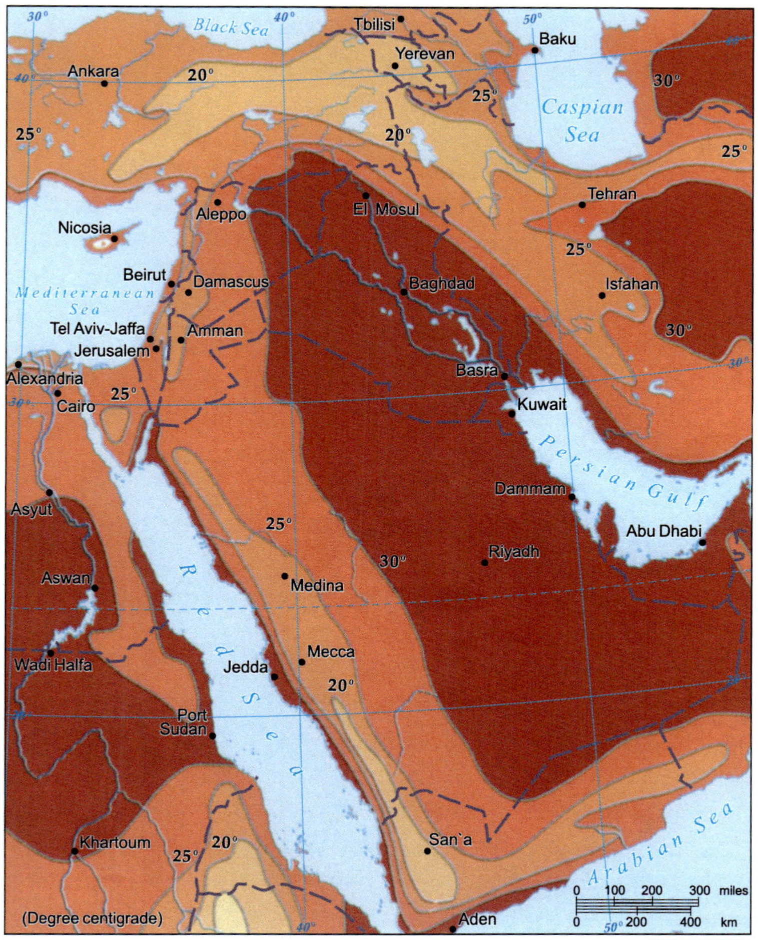

The interplay of sun and rain in Israel's fertile Huleh Basin forms a fitting backdrop for the remains of an Iron Age storehouse at Hazor.

have a more temperate climate both in the summer and winter, for the sea can absorb the sun's rays to a depth of up to 656 feet (200 m) below sea level, thereby moderating temperatures and retaining warmth the year around. The landmasses that are more distant from the sea have a more extreme climate because the soil retains the warmth of the sun's rays only to a depth of 3 to 6 feet (1–2 m) from the surface.

Overall, the climate of the Middle East is quite varied. The central part—Egypt and Arabia, Israel, Syria, and southern Mesopotamia—has a subtropical climate with dry summers and rainy winters, as described above. The southern extremities, however—Ethiopia, Sudan, and Yemen—are characterized by a monsoon climate in which the seasons are reversed: the summers are rainy and the winters dry. As most of the Middle East is covered by or in close proximity to deserts and surrounded by lofty mountains, climatic variations throughout are extreme. However, areas that touch the sea, in particular the Mediterranean, are temperate, wet and warm, and it is here in particular that permanent human settlement has always been most viable.

As for the eastern Mediterranean Basin, the climate is influenced by European rather than Middle Eastern forces, and is moderated by the influence of the sea itself. Throughout the Mediterranean world the sea is the overwhelming natural phenomenon and tends to hold temperatures within each season relatively stable. The differences between the summer and winter, however, can be dramatic. Hot, dry summers are usually offset by wet winter storms that are powered by a combination of hot air from North Africa, moist air from the Atlantic and cold air from the European interior. The eastern seaboard of the Mediterranean, including the land of Israel, is a climatic transitional zone between the wetness of the sea and the dryness of the desert, and where wild fluctuations between "feast and famine" are to be expected.

Because of these climatic extremes, the regions of the biblical world are home to a great variety of flora and fauna, as well as patterns of human settlement. For instance, the foothills and river valleys of northern Persia and Anatolia, covered with primeval forests, have dense human and animal populations, while desert regions such as Rub' al-Khali and Nafud in Arabia are among the most sparsely populated in the world. The region's various climatic boundaries, then, demarcate the parameters of the fertile areas and wasteland regions of the biblical world.

Climatic Regions

The geographic extent of the Middle East, its varied physical structure and the interplay of desert, mountain and sea create six distinct regions of climate, agriculture and possibilities for human settlement:

1. The Pontic climate of Anatolia. The cold and wet Pontus region enjoys more than 40 inches (100 cm) of rain throughout most of the year. This area has the richest forests in the Middle East and supports both irrigated and non-irrigated crops.

2. The interior mountain climate of Armenia. This region, which receives about 20 to 40 inches (50–100 cm) of precipitation annually, is very cold and snowy in the winter and cool in summer. In winter the land completely freezes over, while in summer flocks graze on the mountains and fruit and grain are cultivated in the river valleys.

3. The subtropical climate of the Anatolian and Persian plateaus. This region is very hot and dry in summer and cold and somewhat humid in winter, with 16 inches (40 cm) or less of precipitation annually. Barley and wheat are cultivated and flocks of sheep and goats are raised in the mountains and valleys, while the central salt deserts are completely barren.

4. The Mediterranean climate throughout the eastern Mediterranean Basin. This region has an average of 20 to 40 inches (50–100 cm) of rain in the winter and no rain in the summer. A wide variety of fruit and grain is grown solely on natural rainfall, and cattle, sheep and goats thrive in the valleys and on the hillsides.

5. The desert climate. The deserts of Arabia, Egypt

CLIMATIC REGIONS OF THE MIDDLE EAST

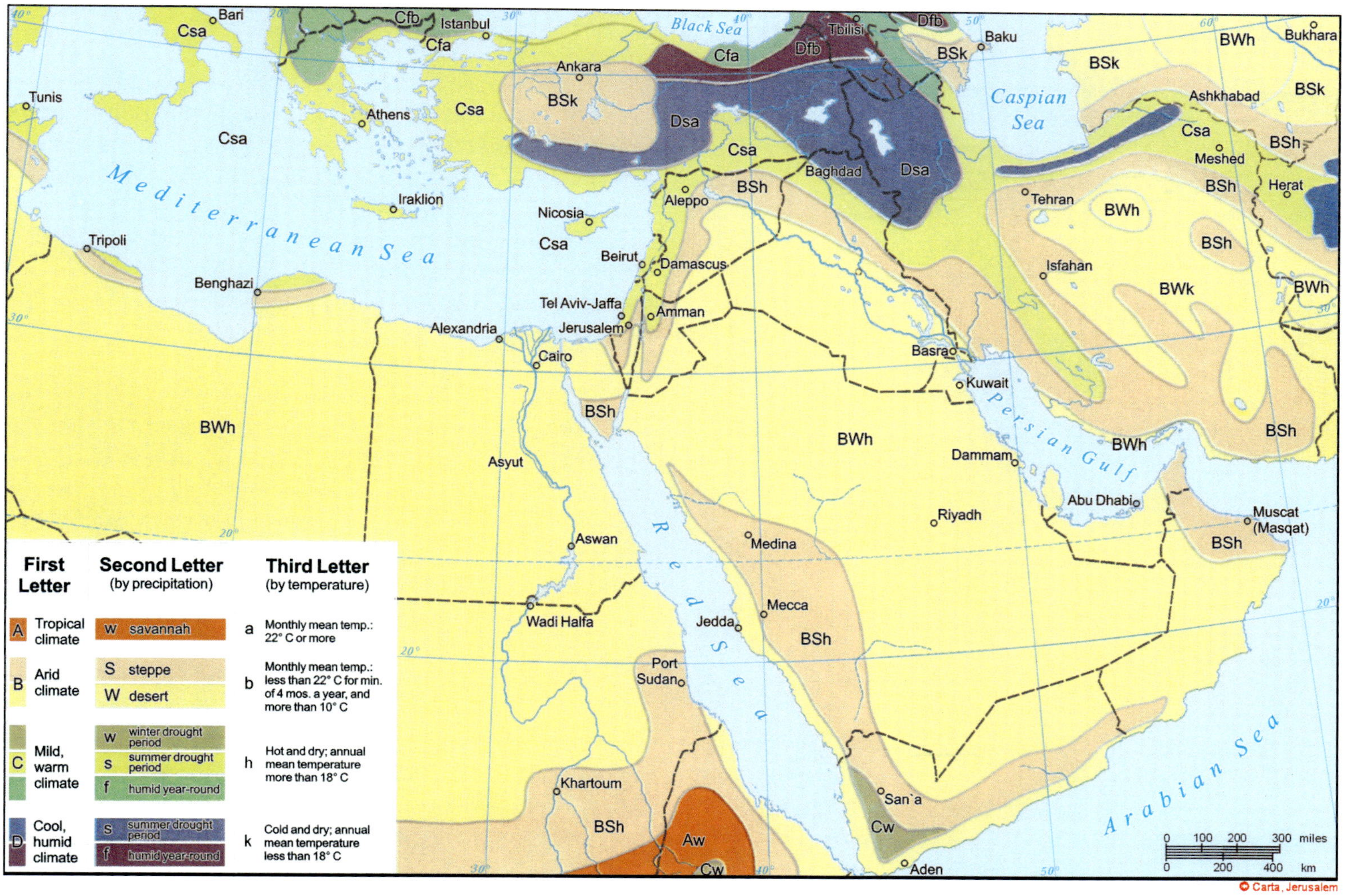

Clouds bearing a hint of winter moisture envelop Jebel Haroun, Petra, one of the most prominent sandstone mountains overlooking the Rift Valley in southern Jordan.

and the southern part of Mesopotamia are dry for most of the year, receiving less than 8 inches (20 cm) of rainfall annually. Crops are irrigated in the river valleys, and desert oases provide homes to sheep, goats and camels.

6. The monsoon climate of Sudan and Yemen. This region receives some 20 to 40 inches (50–100 cm) of rain annually. Here, in antiquity, plants for incense and perfumes were grown under irrigation, and cattle were bred.

PHYSICAL GEOGRAPHY AND HUMAN SETTLEMENT IN THE ANCIENT NEAR EAST

The lands of the ancient Near East included the large river valleys of Egypt and Mesopotamia as well as the rainy hills and valleys of the eastern Mediterranean seaboard. In the history of the ancient world, the countries that filled this Fertile Crescent had outstanding opportunities to establish profitable trading networks, complex social organizations, mature urban centers, sophisticated political institutions, lofty religious ideas, and refined skills in communication, manufacturing and the arts and sciences. Advances in culture spread from the Fertile Crescent to the east by way of Persia (Iran), westward into the Mediterranean Basin, and to the southeast through Canaan and Israel. Many of the factors that spurred these initial advances in human cultural development are rooted in the geographical realities of the ancient Near East: climate, natural resources, routes and the region's overall geographical setting in the known world of the time.

Major Centers of Human Culture

In the most general sense, the ancient Near East can be divided into three distinct geographical regions:

1. A mountainous northern region extending laterally along the boundary of the temperate zone in a generally east-west direction. This fertile region includes the lands of Persia, Anatolia, and, to their south, Mesopotamia.

2. A southern region, located along the boundary of the monsoon zone and extending in a longitudinal north-south direction toward the Red Sea and Nile River. This is a desert region that includes Egypt, Cush (Ethiopia), Arabia, and Yemen.

3. A third, and smaller, zone consists of the lengthy Syrian-African Rift, a long, longitudinal rip in the surface of the earth that in some ways joins the larger northern and southern regions to each other, and in other ways separates them.

Together, these three regions are circumscribed by five seas: the Mediterranean Sea, the Red Sea, the Persian Gulf, the Caspian Sea and the Black Sea. It was here, in a great amphitheater built of mountains, valleys and deserts and surrounded by water, that the world's first civilizations arose. The specific histories of the many peoples who lived in the ancient Near East—the rise and fall of empires, the tenacious cling of individual city-states to their homelands, the migratory patterns of semi-nomadic herders up and down the fringes of the desert—in large measure can be read through the prism of the geographical realities that each faced. Details of climate and fertility may be found in rainfall and available water resources, but these in turn have their roots in larger geological forces that laid the structural foundations of the earth.

PHYSICAL MAP OF THE ANCIENT NEAR EAST

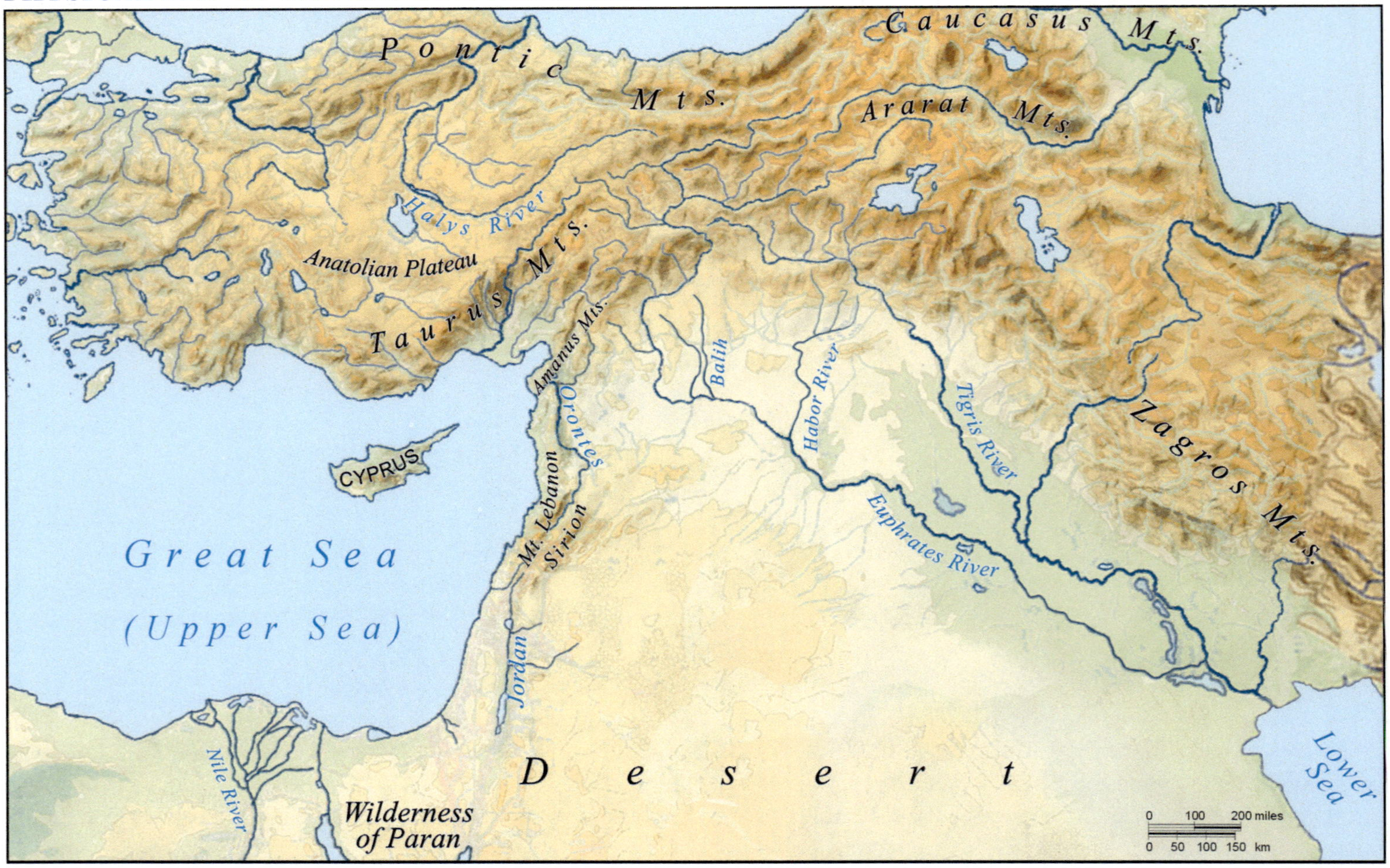

GEOLOGY OF THE MIDDLE EAST

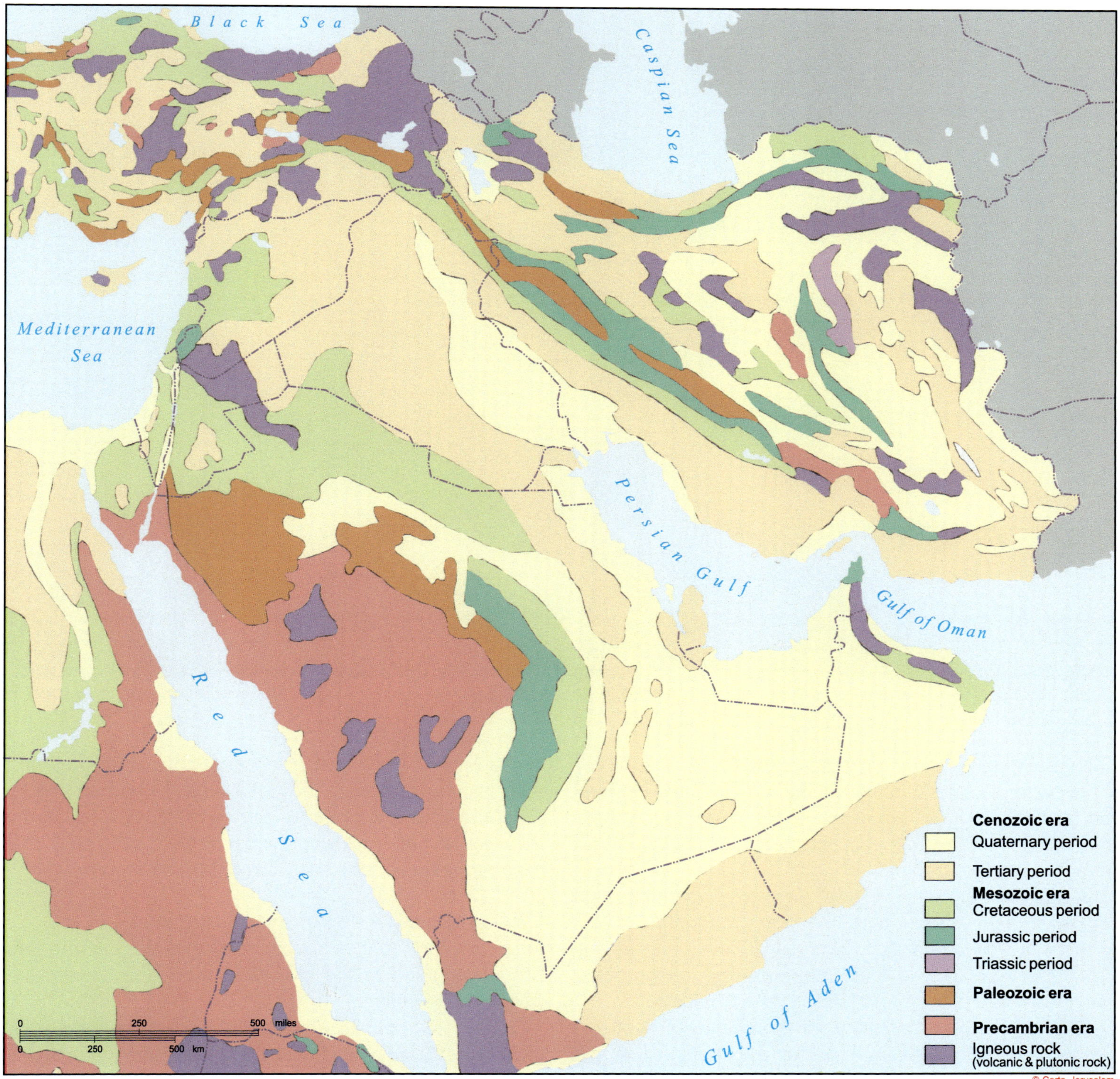

Geological and Tectonic Structure

The Near East can also be divided into three major geological and tectonic structures: (1) ancient massifs (i.e., principal mountain masses); (2) young Alpine folds and faults which were responsible for individual mountains, mountain ranges and valleys; and (3) sandstone and salt plateaus, primarily deserts.

1. Three ancient massifs define the region: the Arabo-Nubian Massif, the Anatolian Massif and the Midian Massif in Persia. Here, in small, protected and well-watered valleys and on rocky yet fertile hillsides, the earliest known villages in the ancient Near East arose. Here, too, ancient man quarried for copper, silver, gold, iron, and semi-precious stones. These metals and gems provided raw materials to make tools, weapons, implements of agriculture and jewelry. Such raw materials not only provided a stimulus for manufacturing but were a catalyst for competition in trade, and at times led to all-out war among the peoples and great nations who sought control of their access.

2. The young Alpine folds raised mountains to heights of 13,100 to 16,400 feet (4,000–5,000 m) above sea level. These include the Pontic and Taurus mountains in Anatolia together with the basalt "seam" in Armenia to their east, the Elburz and Zagros ranges along the border of Mesopotamia and in Persia, the mountains of Yemen and Ethiopia near the Red Sea, and those of Oman in the Persian Gulf.

Mount Hermon forms the southern end of the Anti-Lebanon mountains, a prominent range of folded mountains separating modern Lebanon from Syria.

This folding subsided in the southern margins of the region where a simple, relatively low series of folds formed the backbones of Lebanon and Israel, rising to no more than 9,900 feet (3,000 m) and 3,300 feet (1,000 m), respectively.

Throughout the entire region, mountains were torn and separated by a series of faults, the most prominent of which formed the Syrian-African Rift. The activity of faulting turned areas of simple folds into complex topographies, with jumbled highlands and hidden interior valleys.

3. Other than the homeland of the Hittites high on the central Anatolian plateau, most of the countries in the ancient Near East were surrounded by desolate deserts of sand, gravel or salt. Typical desert plateaus of sandstone are found in Arabia (Rub' al-Khali and Nafud) and, to a lesser degree, Egypt and Sudan. The basalt and flinty desert plateaus in Syria, Arabia, and northern Sinai provide harsh living conditions that lack adequate water resources for permanent human settlement and generally inhibit plant growth. The principal salt plateaus of the Near East, Dasht-e Kavir and Dasht-e Lut in Persia (Iran), and other, smaller ones in areas near Lake Tuz in Anatolia, served as obstacles to both man and beast and were always the most desolate and infertile lands in the entire region.

It can be argued that the best natural border is a desert, for a desert acts as a frontier or barrier between nations and can prevent or deter wars. At the same time, because the deserts of the ancient Near East held important natural resources such as iron, copper, turquoise and high-quality stone for construction or works of art, once the skills of forging trade routes and traversing the desert were harnessed, they became centers of economic or political development.

Characteristics of Folded Mountains

In several ways the mountain ranges of the ancient Near East contributed to the growth of human settlement and culture in the region:

1. The lofty mountains of the northern region in particular receive and store a great amount of precipitation, including snow-cover, in winter and spring. Here crops are watered by rainfall, while natural thickets of oak, pine, beech, fir, cypress, cedar, and other trees flourish, providing lumber for construction and making implements, tools and weapons of war. Throughout antiquity farmers cultivated the slopes and valleys of both the higher mountains in Anatolia and Persia and the lower ranges adjacent to the Mediterranean Sea.

2. From the heights and slopes of the folded mountains flowed the headwaters of the great rivers of the ancient Near East, the Nile and its sources in Cush (Ethiopia) and East Central Africa, and the Tigris and Euphrates with their sources in eastern Anatolia. To a lesser extent we can add to this list the smaller rivers of the Levant: the Orontes and Litani in Aram-zobah (Aleppo) and in the kingdom of Hamath in the Valley of Lebanon; the Abana and Pharpar in

Aram-damascus; and the River Jordan in Israel. In addition, important oases can be found in the desert regions at the foot of these high mountains. Thus, irrigated agriculture became possible in the flat arid lands below the mountains. Egypt and the Mesopotamian countries developed river transportation in papyrus boats, and the rivers formed the principal artery of communication and life within those lands.

3. The folded mountain ranges served as defensive rings, protecting for instance Persia, Anatolia, and Arabia from enemies beyond their frontiers. The ancient capitals of these lands—Susa, Hattusa, Mecca and Medina—were established in interior regions that were surrounded or bordered by high mountains.

4. In the high mountain meadows, ancient man raised flocks of sheep and goats and cultivated grain, products that provided basic food and clothing.

But these mountains held disadvantages for human settlement as well. Perhaps most importantly, the high mountains constitute a barrier against the rain-bearing winds that blow inland from the seas. As a result, the leeward sides of the mountains were arid and tended to lack fertility. In addition, the rugged mountain slopes led to destructive soil erosion, making cultivation here difficult but depositing heavy alluvial soils in the river valleys below. The great height and ruggedness of these mountains also made it difficult to build and maintain good roads, with the result that the heights of the mountains resisted population growth and commercial development.

In the mountains above Mesopotamia, these geographical conditions were adequate for small village farming and herding, but it was only when people moved down to the open Tigris and Euphrates river valleys below, to areas that received the blessing of run-off water and eroded alluvial soil from the mountains above, that the age of true urbanization and empire-building could begin. At the same time, the geographical divisions within the ancient Near East encouraged the establishment of many small, independent city-states and kingdoms in isolated and remote desert and mountainous areas. These smaller nations grew under the shadow of the cultural and religious influences cast by the mighty nations of the day—Babylonia, Assyria, Persia, Egypt, the Hittites, Greece and Rome—rising in their wake and sinking together with them.

The Fertile Crescent

The most important centers of urbanization and culture in the ancient Near East, then, were located along the great river valleys of Mesopotamia and Egypt, while a region of secondary importance lay between them, adjacent to the eastern seaboard of the Mediterranean Sea. This entire area has been called the Fertile Crescent because of its crescent-like shape and the inherent possibilities of the land to support permanent settlement. The soil lying in the

The towering sandstone mountains of Wadi Rum in southern Jordan are typical of the desert landscape of the northern Arabian Peninsula.

THE FERTILE CRESCENT—ANCIENT AND MODERN

Tigris and Euphrates river valleys in Mesopotamia and the Nile river valley in Egypt was very fertile due to the annual heavy deposit of silt brought down from their mountainous headwaters at flood time (autumn in Egypt; spring in Mesopotamia). As the result of irrigation, these arable flood plains could be quite productive. Conversely, the lands of the eastern seaboard of the Mediterranean, including Syria and Israel, owed their agricultural productivity to the winter rainfall carried by the prevailing Mediterranean winds. Here agriculture was less certain than in Egypt or Mesopotamia, but the variety of crops grown nicely complemented those of the great river valleys. The writer of Deuteronomy accurately described this aspect of the Fertile Crescent:

> For the land that you are about to enter and possess is not like the land of Egypt from which you have come. There the grain you sowed had to be watered by your own labors, like a vegetable garden; but the land you are about to cross into and possess, a land of hills and valleys, soaks up its water from the rains of heaven. (Deut 11:10–11)

What conditions were needed for human settlement to take root and grow in the lands of the Fertile Crescent? Four geographic factors contributed to the rise of settlement and subsequent cultural development there:

1. Fertile alluvial soil, warm sunshine during most of the year and a consistent supply of water were of utmost importance. Such conditions exist in the river lands and in the coastal regions of the eastern Mediterranean Sea, but also in the monsoon regions of the Horn of Africa and south Yemen, both lying outside of the Fertile Crescent.

2. The river valleys were afforded natural protection by deserts and mountain ranges.

3. The Euphrates and Nile rivers, and to a lesser extent the faster-flowing Tigris, served as internal avenues of transport linking together the cities and power centers that sprang up among the fertile fields along their banks. From these, land routes connected Egypt to Mesopotamia through the plains and mountain passes of the eastern Mediterranean Coast.

4. Perhaps most significantly for the long run, the political, economic, and commercial importance of the Fertile Crescent lay in the fact that it served as a land bridge between three continents: Africa, Europe and Asia, including the Arabian Peninsula. From many points along its length, land and sea routes radiated into the world beyond. Although the Fertile Crescent was the birthplace of urbanization and true cultural advance, its position between larger world powers east and west eventually caused it to be overrun and its heritage transported to other lands, where it spurred and enriched further cultural development.

Agriculture

Several factors combined to limit large-scale agriculture in the ancient Near East to the river valleys, coastal plains and adjacent intermountain valleys, the plateaus and hills of the Mediterranean region and the mountainous areas of the monsoon lands. All had to do with the adequate retention of arable soil. First, in the mountainous, steep-sloped regions, heavy rainfall and annual flooding scoured soil from the fertile mountainsides and deposited it in valleys, depressions, lakes and seas. Second, desert regions see an intensive negative movement of soil in which dry winds

The Nile River valley receives virtually no rainfall, so fields in rural Egypt must be irrigated, in this case by a water wheel.

move enormous quantities of sand, constantly threatening to cover oases and water sources. Third, the parching effect of the desert climate itself wreaks havoc on the fertility of the soil. As a result, the cultivated areas in the Near East have always been confined to no more than 15 percent of its total land area.

Due to the large number and variety of productive ecosystems in the ancient Near East, the availability of indigenous products, both plant and animal, was extensive. These offered sufficient food for a varied, healthy diet, and material for both durable and elaborate clothing.

For millennia, people inhabiting the lands of the Near East have engaged in three major types of food production:

GEOBOTANICAL REGIONS

1. *Irrigated agriculture*. The large river valleys (Tigris, Euphrates and Nile) and their deltas were extensively irrigated as early as the third millennium B.C., bringing life-giving water to otherwise unproductive, arid soil. The main crops grown in these areas were grain, legumes, vegetables, dates and flax.

2. *Rainfall agriculture and horticulture*. A variety of crops has always been grown in the hilly and mountainous areas throughout the ancient Near East, areas that cannot be irrigated. The principal rainfall crops are orchard crops: grapes, olives, pomegranates, figs and almonds. Grain is also cultivated on plateaus and in valleys throughout the region; the grain fields of Anatolia, Persia, al-Jazirah in Mesopotamia and the Hauran in the east central Levant are particularly productive.

3. *Livestock*. Goats, sheep and donkeys have always been raised along the edges of the desert and along the border between the cultivated areas and the wastelands, in regions that receive between 4 and 8 inches (10 and 20 cm) of rainfall per year, less than the minimum needed for agriculture. Suitable grazing land for cattle can be found throughout the region, in the river valleys and plains where moisture and fresh grass are found throughout the year. In biblical times horses were bred in the steppe regions with natural pasturage, such as Asia Minor. Domesticated camels habit the edge of deserts, where the annual average rainfall is less than 4 inches (10 cm).

A perennial threat facing these lands, wedged as they are between desert, mountain and sea and always tottering

THE ECONOMY OF THE ANCIENT NEAR EAST

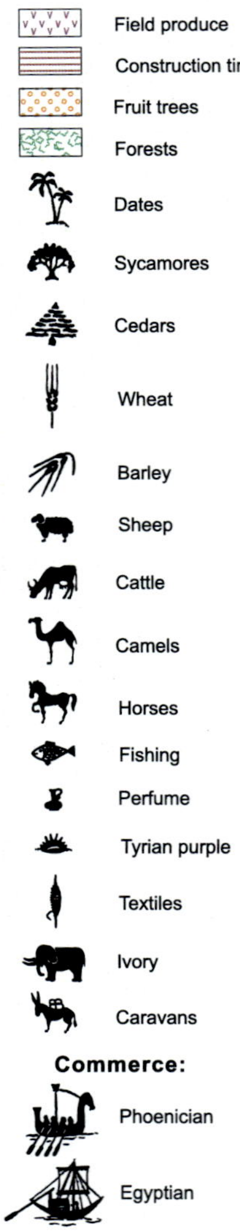

(clockwise, top left) Barley, acacia blossoms, olive trees, wheat.

between feast and famine, was invasion by neighbors whose own crops, flocks or herds had failed. From the point of view of farmers who had plenty, such invaders seemed "like locust for number . . . coming into the land to devastate it" (Judg 6:5). For the one who had to flee lands in the grip of famine, however, the intent was just to survive, to "sojourn" somewhere productive like Egypt until conditions back home improved (Gen 12:10). Clearly, the yearly effects of climate and fertility—the base-line of economic independence and success in the ancient Near East—proved to be points of contention for both individual farmers and herders, and for nations.

Transportation

A line of high, rugged mountain ranges running from the western Himalayas through Persia and Anatolia into the Balkans formed a rugged northern "backbone" for the lands of the ancient world. The overwhelming geographical reality of these mountains largely determined the basic pattern and east-west direction of the road system in the ancient Near East.

Other geographic features affecting the location of routes in the ancient Near East are longitudinal in direction. These

Rainfall is adequate for agriculture in the region of Iznik (ancient Nicea), in northwestern Anatolia.

were created by longitudinal folds and the sinking of the Syrian-African Rift. Mountain ranges in the vicinity of the Syrian-African Rift, namely those of Arabia, Midian, Transjordan, Canaan, Cush and Egypt, tend to run in the same north-south direction as the Rift. The main line of east-west routes met the main line of north-south routes in the northern Levant.

Roads in the ancient Near East gradually developed as a result of international trade, wars between nations, the migration of nomads from region to region, and, eventually, the journeys of pilgrimages to holy sites and shrines. The recurrent challenge faced by nations or individuals bent on journeying into the outside world was how to navigate through the mountains and wastelands in a way that most efficiently and effectively connected one point to the next, and allowed the traveler to return home safely. Natural routes, then, connected main population centers by following areas of least resistance, through mountain passes and over river fords, from water source to water source. Springs found in the foothills of the mountains or in the desert wastelands became oases and meeting places for travelers of all sorts, and those who knew the whereabouts of these water sources or determined who might have access to them *de facto* controlled the entire route.

A number of natural passes threaded the ridges and clefts of the lofty and lower mountain ranges. Among them are the following, each indicated by its modern name: the Tripoli Pass between the Lebanon and Ansariyeh mountains; the Syrian Gates between the Ansariyeh and Amanus mountains; the Cilician Gates through the Bulgar Daglari range in the eastern Taurus Mountains; the Menderes and Gadid passes in western Turkey; the Zonguldak and Trabzon passes on the Black Sea; the Tiflis (Tbilisi) Pass in Armenia between the areas of the Black and Caspian seas; the Rasht and Demavend passes in the Elburz Mountains in Persia; the Zagros Pass between Hamadan in Persia and Baghdad; the Bulan Pass between Persia and Pakistan; the Strait of Hormuz and Büshehr leading from the Persian Gulf to the Makran and eastern Zagros mountains, respectively; the Bir Ali Pass in southern Yemen; and the Jedda Pass on the Red Sea between the Asir and Hejaz provinces in Saudi Arabia. Additional points of access through mountain ranges were natural lowlands or basins that extended inland from the coast, such as the Jezreel Valley and the Beer-sheba Basin of the biblical Negeb. To these we can add four sea passes: the Straits of Bosporus and the Dardanelles connecting the Black Sea with the Mediterranean through the Sea of Marmara; the Strait of Bab el-Mandeb between the Red Sea and the Indian Ocean; and the Strait of Hormuz between the Persian Gulf and the Gulf of Oman.

One of the most significant routes connecting east and central Asia with Mesopotamia and the Mediterranean Sea was the Horse and Silk Road. By the dawn of recorded history in the late fourth millennium B.C., travelers had already discovered metals, primarily tin, along this route, transporting it to Mesopotamia and Egypt. Similarly, the horse was introduced to the West from the steppes of Kirghiz and Turkistan via this route as early as the eighteenth

This Bedouin shepherdess heading home at sundown preserves remnants of an ancient lifestyle that has always been found along the desert fringe of the Fertile Crescent.

Camels have been the preferred mode of long-distance transportation on land routes in the ancient Near East for millennia.

century B.C. The Horse and Silk Route also carried the silk trade from China to the Mediterranean lands from the Roman period onward.

Equally viable to the land routes of the ancient Near East were water routes on its five seas or that followed the course of the Nile or Euphrates rivers. For instance, trade through the Persian Gulf to the fabled lands of Magan and Meluhha, perhaps located somewhere in India or eastern Arabia, brought exotic goods into Mesopotamia, as did Red Sea travelers from Sheba (perhaps Yemen or Ethiopia; 1 Kgs 9: 26–10:13) and other points south.

Five Seas Amid Three Continents

The Near East is unique among regions of the world as a meeting point of continents and seas. Not only does it serve as a hub between Europe, Africa, Asia and the Arabian Peninsula, the region is circled by five great seas, each of which is a doorway to the world beyond. The Near East in fact has been called "the region of the five seas," a reference to the role that the Mediterranean, Black, Caspian and Red seas, together with the Persian Gulf, play on the larger world's geopolitical and economic stage.

Of these five seas, the Caspian Sea is the only one fully enclosed, without a natural outlet to the ocean. In modern times its usefulness has been increased by a series of canals connecting it to the Black Sea by way of the Volga and Don rivers. In the world of the ancient Near East, however, the commercial value of the Caspian Sea as a vehicle of transportation was largely nil, and the east-west configuration of the mountain ranges of Persia directed travel westward, to the Black and Mediterranean seas instead.

While the southern part of the Black Sea has a comfortable climate, its shoreline largely lacks suitable inlets and anchorages, and its storms further hinder shipping. In the past only a few seaports were built along this coast, and even today they are small in number. The Black Sea has a single outlet to the west, through the Sea of Marmara and the Dardanelles; this saltwater passage flows into the Mediterranean Sea and facilitates shipping in that direction.

Ships have plied the Persian Gulf since at least the late fourth millennium B.C. These ships carried trade that originated in India and the southern Arabian Peninsula into Mesopotamia, or, via the Euphrates, to markets in lands bordering the Mediterranean Sea.

On the Red Sea, where the shore is for the most part harsh and desolate, fleets of the kingdoms of Yemen, Cush, and Egypt brought goods destined primarily for the inhabited shores of the Mediterranean. These commercial fleets sailed the Red Sea throughout the biblical period, as evidenced by Egyptian texts from the second millennium B.C., the account of King Solomon and the Queen of Sheba in 1 Kings 10, and the role of Tyre as a trade middleman for the ancient world in the mid-first millennium B.C. (Ezek 27:22–25).

For many reasons the Mediterranean Sea was and remains the heart of the Near Eastern economy, and warrants special consideration below.

THE SYRIAN-AFRICAN RIFT

Introduction

The great similarity between the western coastlines and rock formations of Africa and the eastern coastlines and rock formations of South America led to the discovery of enormous geological rifts parallel to the continents in the bed of the Atlantic Ocean. These coasts and rifts provide evidence that sometime during the geological past, what are now the continents of Africa and South America formed a single landmass. These continents drifted apart when an enormous rift developed in the crust of the earth, creating the Atlantic Ocean. Similarly, within the Syrian-African Rift the continuity in the landscape and ancient rock strata on both sides of the Red Sea and Gulf of Aden suggest that in the early geological eras, Africa and Arabia were one landmass.

It appears that the formation of all of the world's great geological faults and rifts were formed by a combination of various tectonic activities exerted on the surface of the earth. These in turn were a result of vertical pressures emanating from tremendous heat below, which reaches 9,000° F (5,000° C) in the earth's liquid and gaseous core. The main tectonic processes responsible for the shape of the earth's surface are defined below:

1. *Expansion*: a geological process in which, as a result of strain, one landmass drifts away from an adjacent landmass causing it to divide along a lengthwise axis.
2. *Pressure*: a geological process in which one landmass presses upon an adjacent landmass, creating folds in the earth's crust, sinking or elevating portions of it so that it breaks along a lengthwise axis. For instance, the pressure of what is now North Africa upon southern Europe caused a massive fold in the earth's crust, forming the Alps in southern Europe and Atlas Mountains in North Africa, with the enormous depression of the Mediterranean Sea collapsing between the two.
3. *Sinking*: a geological process in which the edges of two landmasses, when drifting from each other, collapse and sink to a great depth. This creates a rift.

Formation and Shifting of the Rift Valley

The Syrian-African Rift is a display case for the many geological activities that occurred along its length. This enormously long and narrow cleft extends, almost continuously but with some breaks, for some 3,730 miles (6,000 km), from southern Turkey to the Zambezi River in Mozambique. The Rift was formed by a series of complex processes over the course of several geological eras. In general terms, opposing pressures from the north-northwest and south-southeast created a series of roughly parallel fault lines, and eventually the surface of the earth lying between them collapsed to great depths. There is evidence from the rock strata that at roughly the same time, parts of the landmass east of the Rift slid north. For instance, in the southern Levant strata of chalky limestone that are found in the area of the Timnah mines in the western Arabah do not appear in the mountains of Edom opposite, but rather in the mountains of Moab northeast of the Dead Sea. Also in the Levant, four geological depressions were formed at right angles to the Syrian-African Rift; these are the Negev Basin, the region of Lower Galilee and Bashan, the Homs-Palmyra Gap and the Antioch Saddle in the far north.

In the geological present, high mountains or cliffs edge much of the Rift, in places rising to a height of 6,560 feet (2,000 m) or more. Many of these contain remnants of an ancient volcanic landscape of basalt and lava, or igneous rocks such as granite. In the Rift's tropical regions in the south (east central Africa) and in areas of ample rainfall in the northern Levant, the soft lava and hard basalt rocks have dissolved and blended with other materials, including limestone, to create fertile soil. In the arid and semi-arid portions of the subtropical regions (northeast Africa, the Arabian Peninsula and the southern Levant), these rocks have largely resisted disintegration into soil, and the windswept landscape, composed of stony, barren ground, is typically inhabited by semi-nomads. Portions of the Rift

PRINCIPAL GEOLOGICAL FEATURES

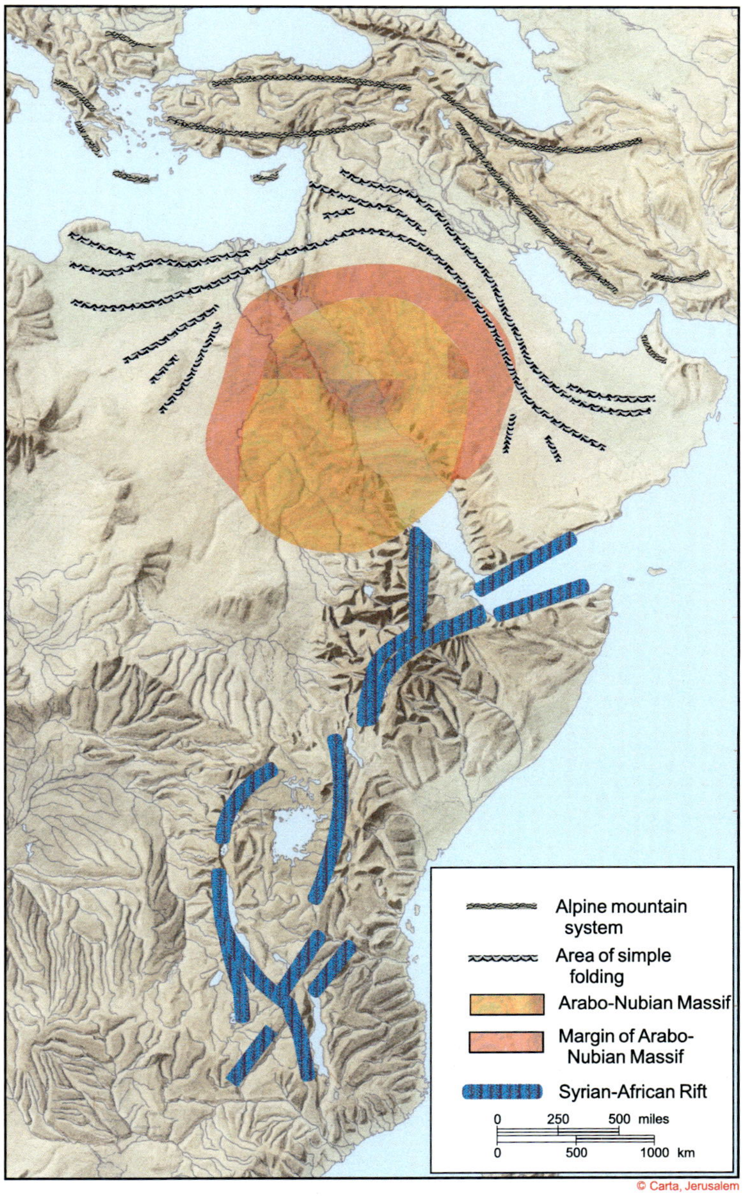

The northern, higher portions of the Rift Valley in the Levant, such as this area just north of Metulla, Israel, are quite fertile.

(below) The southern, lower portions of the Rift Valley in the Levant are among the driest and most inhospitable areas on earth, such as the wilderness rising from the southern end of the Dead Sea.

itself form dry valleys, such as the Arabah in the southern Levant, while other places in the Rift have become riverbeds (e.g. the Jordan, Litani and Orontes rivers). The lowest spots of the Rift have filled with runoff rainwater and the output of rivers (the Sea of Galilee, the Dead Sea and the Great Lakes of east central Africa), or, in the case of the Red Sea, by an elongated arm of the Indian Ocean. The Rift remains geologically active, and places along its vast length are still centers of volcanic or earthquake activity.

In terms of human activity, the Syrian-African Rift has served as an important transportation and migratory route between Africa, Asia and Europe. The four geological depressions that cross the Rift at right angles are conveniently spaced at equal distances along the length of the Levant; together, they provide passes through the cleft of the Rift and its high parallel mountain ranges enabling the routes from Mesopotamia to connect with those of the Mediterranean Sea.

THE LEVANT

Introduction

Largely because of its highly dissected topography, the eastern Mediterranean seaboard has always been home to a number of independent-minded people groups who tend to resist politically unification. It is therefore difficult to assign a single name to this entire region; rather, in the historic period each area has typically taken its local name from the people who lived there. For much of its biblical history, the names "Canaan" and then "Israel" were dominant in the southern, drier half of the land, while in the more fertile north the west was called "Lebanon" or "Phoenicia" and the east "Aram" or "Syria." The Roman term "Palestina," in various forms, designated the entire land during the early centuries A.D. For convenience, it is perhaps easiest to call the entire region the Levant, a modern term which solves the problem of ancient nomenclature.

In spite of its many subregional differences, the Levant constitutes a single geographical unit of mountains and local deserts that run parallel to, and are squeezed between, the Mediterranean Sea and the upper reaches of the Arabian Desert. From south to north, the extent of the region is described by the biblical phrase "from the River of Egypt [probably the Wadi el-Arish in the mid-Sinai] to the Euphrates" (2 Kgs 24:7; cf. 1 Kgs 4:21). The northern part of the region is rainy and the soil is fertile, while deserts such as the Negeb (Gen 20:1), Shur (Ex 15:22), Sin (Ex 16:1), Sinai (Ex 19:2), Paran (Num 12:16) and Zin (Num 21:1) predominate in the far south. The width of the land is defined by two natural boundaries: the "Great Sea" (i.e., the Mediterranean; Num 34:6) to the west and the desolate deserts of Transjordan and Arabia to the east; in the Bible these deserts are called "Kedem" or the "land of the Kedemites" (i.e., the Easterners [Gen 25:6, 29:1]). With the effects of Mediterranean rainfall dominating the north and west and arid deserts lining the east and south, landscape and fertility, as well as options for human sustenance, change dramatically as one travels from the fertile agricultural lands of the northwest to the dry shepherd lands of the southeast.

The defining physical feature of the Levant is the Rift Valley and its two parallel mountain ranges, one lying to the west (the "backbone" of Lebanon and Israel) and the other to the east (the highlands of Syria and Transjordan). The western (Lebanon and Cisjordanian) range begins in the high Amanus Mountains in north Syria and gradually diminishes in elevation along the mountains of Lebanon and Israel until it reaches the Red Sea, then rises dramatically again in the southern Sinai. The eastern (Anti-Lebanon and Transjordanian) range is also generally higher in the north and maintains a height significantly above that of the mountains of Israel in the south before joining the soaring range that lines the western shore of the Arabian Peninsula.

The Mediterranean coastal plain near the ancient Philistine city of Ekron remains one of the most fertile regions of the Levant.

MAJOR ROUTES AND PHYSICAL FEATURES OF THE HOLY LAND

The low, rolling foothills and broad agricultural valleys of the Shephelah provide ample resources for settled life.

The western slopes of each of these ranges are wet and fertile, while the leeward slopes lie in a dry rain shadow. The international routes that bisect the region and join Mesopotamia and Europe with Egypt parallel these lines of mountains. This route tracks along the eastern base of the Anti-Lebanon range, then splits into two branches south of Mount Hermon: the "Way of the Sea" (Isa 8:23) following the Mediterranean coast and the "King's Highway" (Num 20:17) along the crest of the Transjordanian mountains in the east. For millennia these routes have tied the lands of the Levant to larger powers in the north and south, carrying opportunities for economic growth but also the threat of invasion. The four east-west geological depressions mentioned above, the Negeb Basin, the lowlands of Galilee, the Homs-Palmyra Gap and the Antioch Saddle, have served as historical corridors binding west to east. Through these passes the peoples of the Levant have benefited from trade flowing between the lands of the Mediterranean and those of Mesopotamia and Arabia, but by them they also faced invasion from the eastern desert (e.g. Judg 6:1–3).

The Natural Division of the Southern Levant

In biblical writings, the southern part of the Levant is divided into two major regions separated by the Syria-African Rift (here called the Jordan Valley and the Arabah): "the west side of the Jordan" (Josh 12:7), and "the east side of the Jordan" (Josh 13:27), or, "beyond the Jordan" (Deut 1:1; Judg 5:17; Mk 3:8). This division can be further subdivided into five secondary regions, each differing in its rock strata, climate, soil, economy and inhabitants. From west to east, these secondary regions are:

1. *The coastal plain.* Known in the Bible as "the coast of the Great Sea" (Josh 9:1), the coastal plain was inhabited in biblical times by Canaanites (Num 13:29) and Philistines, as well as larger powers such as Egypt, Assyria, Babylon, Persia, Greece and Rome, all who sought to control its port cities and the international route that ran its length. Here

The hill country of biblical Judah and Israel supports a village life dependent on agricultural products that are most suited to rocky mountain terraces: grapes, figs, pomegranates, olives, and almonds (see Deuteronomy 8:8).

The rock-cut tombs of Petra in southern Transjordan bear silent witness to the prosperity of the region during the first century A.D., when the city was an important terminal on the Nabatean Spice Route.

the coastline is straight and relatively free of inlets that might be suitable for heavy Mediterranean vessels, other than at Dor in the Sharon area and Acco/Ptolemais in Galilee. The coastal plain broadens in the south toward the Negeb and Judah, and narrows as one proceeds northward through Sharon and Galilee. Two or three low ridges of soft sandstone (*kurkar*) rising from 100 to 200 feet (30–60 m) in height run the length of the coastal plain, but are more prominent in the Sharon area than in the south. When cut into blocks, this sandstone is fairly durable as a building material and was used to construct houses and public buildings in cities along the coast such as Dor, Caesarea and Ashkelon. In terms of agriculture, the coastal plain was cultivated for grain and flax in biblical times.

2. *The Shephelah*, or lowland (Josh 11:16). This region of soft limestone and chalky hills rising between 500 and 1,500 feet (150 and 450 m) above sea level is located between the coastal plain and the higher hill country of Judah to the east. The rocky hills of the Shephelah are good for grazing, and the valleys are well suited for grain (Judg 15:5). The limestone of the Shephelah is too soft to be used as durable building material, but the hills are covered by a hard, limey crust of *nari* that was used to build fortified cities such Lachish and Gezer. The Shephelah receives runoff rainwater from the higher Judean hills to the east, and the broad valleys through which this water flows to the coast became the focal point of a rich agricultural village life in the region. These valleys also served as local routes carrying traffic between the Judean hill country and the coast. The Shephelah was coveted by the kings in Jerusalem who needed access to its agricultural land and routes, but also by the inhabitants of the coast as they sought to expand eastward. The Samson narrative (Judg 13–16) and the story of David and Goliath (1 Sam 17) best illustrate this geopolitical dynamic. Small areas of the Shephelah are also found in the Mount Carmel range and the foothills east of the coastal plain in Galilee.

3. *The hill country*, also called "the hill country of Israel" (Josh 11:16, 11:21), and, locally, "the hill country of Ephraim" (Josh 24:33) or "the hill country of Judah" (Josh 11:21). Initially populated by Amorites (Num 13:29), this range of hard limestone hills constitutes the central "backbone" of the land. Its elevation varies: the highest points are 3,963 feet (1,208 m) at Meron in Galilee, 3,333 feet (1,016 m) at Baal-hazor in Samaria, 3,369 feet (1,027 m) at Hebron in Judah and 3,379 feet (1,030 m) at Rosh Ramon in the Negeb. The rainfall at such heights is plentiful, and the water-holding capacity of the hard limestone hills provides many useful springs. The fertile soil of the terraced hillsides in the hill country is excellent for grape vines (Isa 5:1) and orchard crops (olives, figs, pomegranates and almonds). This is also an area that enjoys natural defenses: rugged hills and deep valleys face the west, while the desolate Judean Wilderness, the land of the shepherd, drops off to the east. These defenses protect the best agricultural

land and the major cities of the hill country, all of which are balanced along the top of the watershed ridge (Hebron, Bethlehem, Jerusalem, Gibeon and Bethel) or nestled in valleys protected by the hills (Shechem, Shiloh, Tirzah and Samaria).

The hard limestone and basalt hills of Lower Galilee, the region of Galilee that lies between Acco and the Sea of Galilee (the Kinneret), are relatively low (generally less than 1,700 ft./520 m) and open, with wonderful fertile valleys and easy highway access. To the north, Upper Galilee merges with the high hills of Lebanon, areas that are well-watered but favor small, isolated villages due to the ruggedness of the terrain.

4. *The Jordan Valley*. The section of the Syrian-African Rift through which the Jordan River flows is the lowest surface depression in the Levant, dropping to 1,312 feet (400 m) below sea level at the river's entrance to the Dead Sea. What is called the Jordan Valley today was called the Arabah (lit. "desert plain") in the Bible (Josh 18:18; 2 Kgs 25:4); similarly, the Dead Sea was called the Sea of the Arabah (Deut 3:17; Josh 3:16). The southern extension of the Rift between the Dead Sea and the Red Sea is referred to as the Arava today, and apparently that region also bore the same name during the biblical period (Deut 2:8).

The plains of the Jordan provide areas for crop cultivation (Gen 13:10). Because rainfall throughout the Jordan Valley is sparse, most crops need some form of irrigation and so in biblical times were grown at the outlet of springs (especially around Jericho, the "city of palm trees"; Deut 34:3; Judg 3: 13) or streams that flowed out of the hills on either side of the valley. The most extensively irrigated of the plains were in the northern half of the Jordan Valley: the plain at the southern end of the Sea of Galilee, the plain around Beth-shean west of the river, and that at the mouth of the Yarmuk and Jabbok rivers in the east. During the biblical period, flax, balm and dates were grown successfully in these regions.

5. *The Transjordanian highlands*. The mountains in the southern Levant east of the Syrian-African Rift became home to a number of peoples who established kingdoms at the same time that Israel and Judah formed viable states in the west. These were the kingdoms of Assyria (which encroached into Bashan), Ammon (with eyes toward the rain-rich hills of Gilead), Moab and Edom, people who were as suspicious of those living west of the Jordan as Israel and Judah were of them. All-in-all, the elevations east of the Rift were higher than those to the west: these include Mount Hermon at 9,232 feet (2,814 m), Mount Bashan (of the Druse) at 5,692 feet (1,735 m), Mizpeh of Gilead (Jebel Um ed-Daraj) at 4,091 feet (1,247 m), Jebel Dabab in southern Moab at 4,265 feet (1,300 m), and Jebel Mubarakh in Edom at 5,666 feet (1,727 m). These peaks, even in southern Edom, can be snow-covered in winter. From them four perennial rivers flow into the Rift: the Yarmuk in Bashan, the Jabbok in Gilead, and the Arnon and Zered in Moab.

Variations in climate, soil and landforms throughout Transjordan play a large role in shaping the particular subsistence base of each region. In Bashan in the rainy north, a broad band of arable black basaltic soil provides excellent fields for grain, and during the Roman period much of the grain from this region was shipped to other lands in the Mediterranean. Bashan is also known for its cattle-grazing land (Ps 22: 12; Amos 4:1). The high, hard limestone Dome of Gilead supports vines and fruit trees typical of the hill country of Israel lying immediately across the Jordan to the west. Balm from Gilead was prized for its medicinal properties (Jer 8: 22); its modern identification remains uncertain. The high, flat and chalky plateau of Moab, east of the Dead Sea, was known in biblical times as prime grazing land for sheep and goats (2 Kgs 3:4), and although its climate borders on being arid, this land can produce large crops of grain. Farther south, in Edom, the extent of arable land narrows considerably. Although this region's high altitude (Obad 3) usually attracts enough rain for a minimum grain harvest, its economic base is grounded in shepherding (Isa 34:5–7) and control of the northern end of the Arabian Spice Route.

By the time of the New Testament, Greco-Roman culture had taken deep root in the Levant. Cities such as Pella in Transjordan helped to hold Rome's eastern frontier, both militarily and culturally.

EGYPT

Introduction

Egypt was the outstanding oasis of the ancient Near East and the natural bridge into Africa from Asia and the lands of the Mediterranean. In addition, Egypt was the only great power of the Fertile Crescent that was almost entirely surrounded by desert. Its entire existence and economy depended solely on the lengthy Nile River; "Egypt is an acquired country, the gift of the Nile," the historian Herodotus would say in the fifth century B.C. Today, Egypt is 95 percent desert land; in ancient times, the remaining 5 percent, the Nile valley and delta, *was* Egypt. The ancient Egyptians called their land Kemet, "the black land," after the rich color of its soil, and the surrounding wasteland Deshret, "the red land."

The Nile River historically has given Egypt two distinct advantages for agriculture: an abundance of water and a ready supply of soil. The Nile discharges on average 21 billion gallons of water per year. This is fed by perennial rain in the equatorial zone, most of which originates in the monsoon rains of Ethiopia and by rainfall formed by evaporation from Sudan's marshes. Before the construction of the Aswan dams in the last century, the Nile would typically flood its banks during the summer months to a height of over 20 feet (6 m). Not only would this distribute water throughout the canals and backwashes of the Nile Valley, it would also annually fructify the soil by leaving a fresh deposit of rich organic material and leaching out unwanted salts. Thus, Egypt was the cradle of the ancient Near East for cultivation of grain and flax and, in the modern period, also cotton.

Like the Tigris and Euphrates rivers in Mesopotamia, the Nile brings fertility and life to an otherwise arid land.

THE NILE DELTA

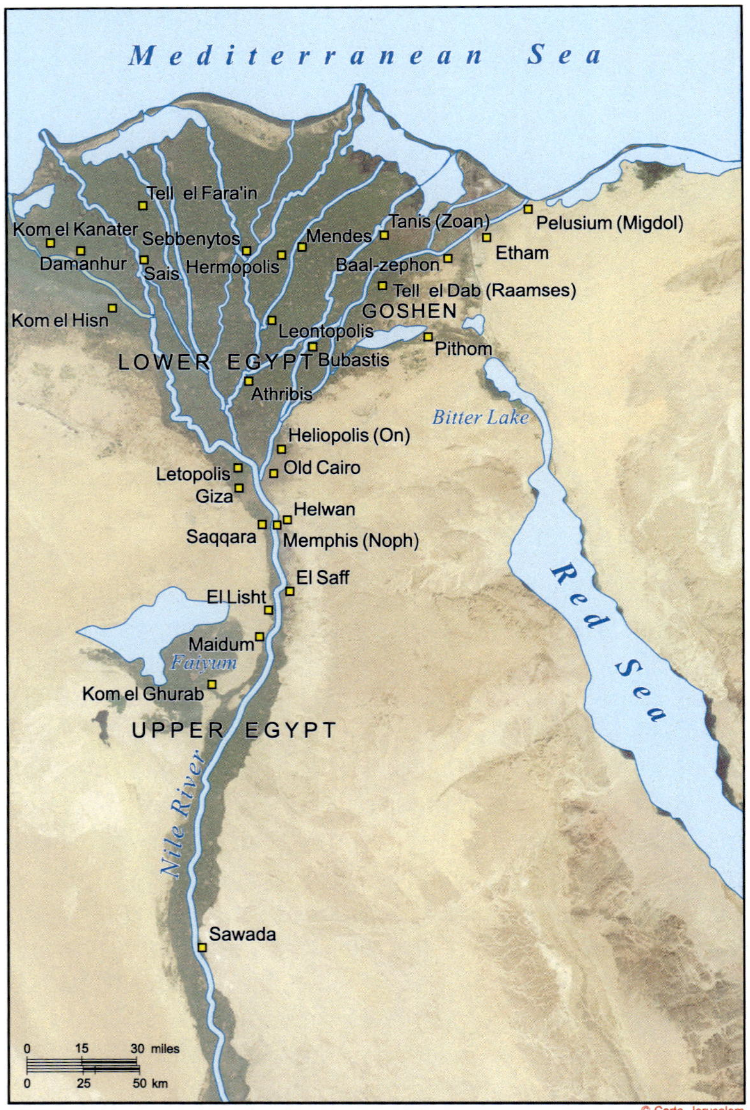

The Nile, which crosses the entire width of the eastern Sahara Desert, flows alternatively through regions of hard limestone, granite and dolomite. In places, these rocks create a series of rapids, or cataracts, that provide a natural defense against attacks by ship from the south. In fact, the Nile's six cataracts tended to separate peoples and lands along the length of the river: in the deep south lay the wet, fertile highlands of Ethiopia, with natural resources of gold, incense and perfume; to the near south was Nubia, fabled in the ancient world for its supplies of gold; and above the first cataract at modern Aswan lay Egypt itself.

Vast stretches of hostile and inhospitable land crowd both sides side of the Nile Valley. In the Western Desert a series of small, scattered oases led to the Libyans, Egypt's ancient enemy to the west. Eastward, a relatively narrow band of rocky desert fronted the high band of mountains bordering the Red Sea, with the Sinai and Arabian deserts beyond. Canaan, across the Sinai to the northeast, offered Egypt the best land and sea link to the world beyond via shipping routes along the Mediterranean coast and land routes running parallel to the shore. In all, access into Egypt was quite difficult from the west, south and east, with the northeastern corridor through Canaan the only viable connection to the greater world. In fact, most invasions into Egypt came from the north, both over land and by sea, and it was through Sinai and Canaan that the New Kingdom pharaohs launched Egyptian imperialism upon the world.

Settlement

Internally, Egypt is divided into two natural regions:

1. *Lower Egypt*, from the Mediterranean to the southern tip of the delta. Because of its large, contiguous size, this was the cradle of Egyptian agriculture. In ancient times the

Nile split into multiple branches below Memphis (modern Cairo), with numerous canals and lines of communication. Perhaps because all areas of the delta are so self-sufficient, this region has tended to fracture into competing centers of power. Important towns include Memphis (Hos 9:6) and On or Heliopolis (Jer 43:13) in the south; Bubastis (Ezek 30:17), Raamses (Ex 1:11) and Zoan (= Tanis; Num 13:22) in Goshen, the eastern delta; and Sais in the western delta. These population centers were concentrated along the branches of the Nile at some distance from the Mediterranean, partly because of the difficulty of exercising control over the marshes that were fed by the Nile but also out of fear of invasion and piracy from the sea. Indeed, the only important city on the coast until Alexander the Great founded Alexandria was Sin-Pelusium, the "stronghold of Egypt" on the northeastern corner of the delta. During Pharaonic times, Lower Egypt was symbolically identified with the cobra and the papyrus.

2. *Upper Egypt*, the narrow length of the Nile Valley from Memphis to Syene (Ezek 29:10, 30:6; today's Aswan at the first cataract). It was this part of Egypt that was most isolated from the rest of the world. Despite the length of their land, the people of Upper Egypt tended to remain unified. Important towns were No-amon or Thebes (modern Luxor; Jer 46: 25; Nah 3:8) and Akhetaten (the site of Tell el-Amarna in the central Nile Valley). Ancient Egyptians symbolically identified Upper Egypt with the vulture and the lotus.

Three times in its long history—during the Old, Middle and New Kingdoms—forces within ancient Egypt forged political unity in the entire land, each time by a pharaoh from Upper Egypt. While the perennial religious capital was at Thebes in Upper Egypt, the political capital tended to move with expediency. Memphis, the first capital of united Egypt, was perhaps the most logical choice for a political capital since it sat at the juncture between north and south. The pharaohs of the New Kingdom built their royal cities in the eastern delta in and around the land of Goshen (Ex 1:11), from which they launched massive campaigns of conquest into Asia. The biblical account of Israel in Egypt finds its setting in this context of Egyptian imperialism.

The assured fertility of the Nile River valley provided an economic basis for ancient Egypt that spurred monumental building projects such as the Pyramids, and fueled an army that in the late second millennium B.C. was the most powerful on earth.

Economic Conditions

Ancient Egypt was rich in irrigated grain crops such as wheat and rye, from which the two staples of the Egyptian diet, bread and beer, were made. To grain we can add a variety of vegetables, including beans, lentils, onions, leeks,

Natural geographical barriers protected ancient Egypt on all sides: Nile cataracts to the south, the Mediterranean to the north, high mountains and the Red Sea to the east and the sandy Sahara, shown here, to the west.

The ancient Egyptians learned to mine the hidden treasures of the desert, such as turquoise at Serabit el-Khadem, here in southwest Sinai.

cucumbers and garlic (Num 11:5), and fruit such as dates, figs, pomegranates and mandrakes, which were also irrigated. Grapevines were cultivated in the delta, although not extensively, and provided wine only for the rich. The Egyptian diet was protein-rich in fish caught from the Nile, its canals and backwater lakes, from brackish marshes along the seacoast and from the salt waters of the Mediterranean and Red seas. In addition, geese and ducks were raised in the Nile and its canals, while cattle, pigs, sheep and goats grazed on lush Nile grass. Non-consumptive crops included flax for linen, and papyrus. Farmers used oxen for plowing and threshing, and donkeys as beasts of burden. The horse arrived in Egypt only at the beginning of the eighteenth century B.C. with the coming of the Hyksos; within a short time it became an indispensable tool of war. The Bible notes Egypt's role in international horse-trading in the time of King Solomon (1 Kgs 10:28–29).

Alabaster, granite and dolomite were quarried from the Eastern Desert, and some limestone and sandstone were cut from cliffs along the Nile. The harder stones were reserved for statues, artwork and religious objects, while limestone and sandstone were used to construct temples and tombs. For reasons rooted in the Egyptian religious world view, it was important for structures related to eternity to be built to last; by contrast, palaces, governmental administrative buildings, public storehouses and common houses were all made of mudbrick. Lumber for shipbuilding and as construction material for elaborate buildings was imported from the northern Levantine coast. Egyptians tapped mines of copper and turquoise in the Sinai, but had to import gold from Nubia and semi-precious stones such as carnelian and lapis-lazuli from the mountains north of Persia.

By far the easiest means of transport in ancient Egypt was along the Nile and its branches in the delta. Boats moving northward were carried along by the currents; southward travel was aided by the northern winds that blow steadily from the Mediterranean. Skill in river navigation encouraged the use of sailboats on the open sea as well. Egyptian mariners sailed to Phoenicia, Crete and Cyprus to bring back lumber, metals, and agricultural products. They sailed the Red Sea for perfumes, incense, gold, frankincense, and ivory. The prophet Isaiah heard of Egyptian ships "which send envoys by the sea, even in papyrus vessels on the surface of the waters" (Isa 18:2).

From the earliest days of recorded history the farmers of Egypt have been able to grow a surplus of food. This encouraged urbanization, which in turn prompted unification of the country and the development of formal trading networks within Egypt itself, then with neighboring lands in Africa, Asia and the Mediterranean Basin. At the same time, the lack of some basic resources served as both an excuse and an impetus to invade these same neighbors. Throughout its history Egypt looked covetously at its adjacent and more distant neighbors—and they at it—and long periods of peaceful trade were invariably broken by campaigns of conquest.

Egyptian merchant ship from the days of Hatshepsut, c. 1500 B.C.

MESOPOTAMIA

Introduction

The word "Mesopotamia" refers, literally, to land lying "between the rivers." This term was first coined by the Greek writers Polybius (second century B.C.) and Strabo (first century A.D.) to refer to the land lying between the Euphrates and Tigris, in particular where their courses draw together above the Persian Gulf. Some modern historians suggest that perhaps "Mesopotamia" is better understood to reflect the Hebrew term "Aram-Naharaim," the land lying between the upper reaches of the Euphrates and its important northern tributary, the Habor River, which includes the region of Haran and Nahor of the patriarchal narratives (Gen 11:27, 11:31–32, 24:10). Be that as it may, most scholars are comfortable to speak in more general terms and label as Mesopotamia that land which lies between the Mediterranean Sea and the Persian Gulf, and between the rugged Zagros Mountains to the north and northeast and the vast reaches of the Arabian Desert to the south and southwest. In spite of these geographical boundaries, most of which might at first appear to provide natural defenses, the lands of Mesopotamia were invaded and ruled by various ethnic peoples intermittently throughout their long history. In fact, due to its location as a corridor connecting east and west and combined with an intrinsic economic advantage that derives from the water and fertility of the Tigris and Euphrates river systems, Mesopotamia became both the cradle of civilization and a major crossroads of the ancient Near East.

The Tigris and Euphrates rivers, yielding on average 19 billion gallons of water per year, flow through the Mesopotamian plain. Of this the Bible says: "O you who dwell by many waters, rich in treasures..." (Jer 51:13). Thus the lands of Mesopotamia produce a variety of agricultural crops watered both by natural rainfall and irrigation, and support animal husbandry. The area's economic wealth, based on the fertility of its land, led to the development of important cities at the dawn of history.

The landforms of Mesopotamia, much more varied than those of Egypt, can be divided into five natural regions:

1. The delta. This is the lower, southeastern corner of Mesopotamia, just above the Persian Gulf. Here the kingdom of Sumer arose. The delta marshes adjacent to the Gulf appear to have been the ancestral home of the Chaldeans.

2. The plain where the Tigris and Euphrates rivers converge. This was the seat of the kingdoms of Accad (Gen 10:10) and Babylon (Jer 51:13–14), and the region to which the Jews were taken into exile (Ps 137:1).

The remains of Nimrud (Calah), lower left, with the Tigris River in the background.

3. The Jazirah. This is the heights above the convergence of the Tigris and Euphrates and the seat of the kingdom of Mitanni.

4. The foothills of the Zagros Mountains. From here streams feed into the Tigris River. The ancient kingdoms of Elam (Gen 14:1, 14:9) and the Kassites were centered on the southern Zagros foothills and the plain below, while Asshur (Gen 10: 22), or Assyria, arose in the foothills of the northern Zagros Mountains.

5. The southern Syrian and Arabian deserts, from which various Semitic tribes entered Mesopotamia.

It is important to note that the two best known Mesopotamian kingdoms, Assyria and Babylonia, found their respective homelands at opposite ends of the confluence of the Tigris and the Euphrates rivers. These rivers, which together form the natural transportation artery of Mesopotamia, differ in their characteristics and somewhat in their direction of flow. The Euphrates originates in the mountains of Ararat and Pontus in Anatolia. It flows first in a south-southwesterly direction to a point within 100 miles (160 km) of the Mediterranean where it connects with an important land route through the Antioch Saddle to that sea, then bends southeast for its long, somewhat sluggish run to the Persian Gulf. In this the Euphrates plays a unique role in the ancient Near East, joining the main bodies of water west and east. The Euphrates has two primary tributaries, the Balik River on whose banks sat Haran, from where the Patriarchs set out for the land of promise (Gen 12:5), and the Habor River, to which the king of Assyria exiled the inhabitants of Samaria (2 Kgs 17:6).

The Tigris River (Gen 2:14) descends from the Zagros Mountains near the cities of Nineveh (Gen 10:11), Calah (Gen 10:11) and Asshur in several fast-moving tributaries. It runs roughly parallel to the lower half of the Euphrates before discharging into it just above the Persian Gulf. The Tigris flows faster and more erratically than does the Euphrates, and the lands along its banks have always been more susceptible to flooding. Much of the flat alluvial plain lying between the two rivers, from the point where they first come to within 25 miles (40 km) of each other (modern Baghdad) until the point that they enter the Persian Gulf 250 miles (400 km) downstream, has for millennia been laced with manmade canals (e.g. the Chebar; Ezek 1:3), providing one of the greatest agricultural breadbaskets of the ancient world.

History and Settlement

Ancient agriculture did not originate in the river valleys of Mesopotamia, where superior administrative skills and technological organization was needed in order to control the Tigris and Euphrates so that the plain between them could be irrigated, but in the high Zagros Mountains to the north and east. These mountains rise 2,625 to 5,250 feet (800–1,600 m) above sea level and receive from 10

Satellite photo showing Oman, the Straits of Hormuz, the Persian Gulf, and part of the Zagros Mountains of Iran.

to 24 inches (25–60 cm) of rainfall each winter, conditions sufficient for rainfall agriculture. The early inhabitants of these mountains lived a peaceful life and over time learned how to domesticate livestock and cultivate wild grain. The population slowly changed from food-gatherers to food-producers. Farming villages dating from the Neolithic period (the New Stone Age, beginning around 7000 B.C.) have been found at Jarmo, in the Zagros Mountains of Kurdistan. In the fifth millennium B.C., these early farmers descended from the mountains to the valleys of Mesopotamia and began to cultivate irrigated crops. Only in the fourth millennium, during the Chalcolithic period (Copper Age), were cities first built in Mesopotamia and nations and kingdoms first established in the river valleys.

The impetus for urban development in Mesopotamia was the cultivation of crops under irrigation from the waters of the rivers that flowed throughout the year. In the winter the tributaries of the Euphrates and Tigris are fed by rainfall, and by the beginning of the summer the snow on the mountains melts and provides abundant runoff. Once the technology was developed for channeling the water as irrigation water, it became possible to grow surplus crops and support an increasingly large population. Success at farming and animal husbandry, and a ready accessibility to trade routes along the river valleys, provided a source of wealth for the inhabitants of Mesopotamia, spurring the rise of towns, then cities and urban life.

As a result of various social factors, including a division of labor and a re-channeling of human endeavors from basic subsistence activities to other pursuits, these early civilizations witnessed a flowering of creative activities in literature, religion and the arts, as well as rudimentary attempts to understand and control the natural world through technology and what is called today "science." For instance, the farmer's observation of the growth patterns of the flora and fauna planted seeds that would lead to the development of biology. Ease of transportation along the flat river valleys and the need to harness the benefits of the water prompted the development of the wheel, cart, pulley and, eventually, the water wheel, all based on principles of physics. Control of the rivers' water flow through dams and canals led to advances in engineering and architecture. Observation of the heavenly bodies, the rise and fall of waters in the rivers and Persian Gulf, and the seasons of the agricultural year spurred the development of astrology and then astronomy. All this led to an early understanding of sophisticated mathematics and to the creation of a calendar to accurately mark and predict the passage of time. At the same time, the inhabitants of ancient Mesopotamia felt a close connection to the world of the divine as it was seen to manifest itself in natural phenomena: the sun, moon and stars, wind and rain, mountains and rivers. The combination of religious and rudimentary scientific understandings of the world around them helped to make the Sumerians, and eventually the Assyrians and Babylonians, carriers of a great religious tradition that influenced the entire ancient Near East and beyond. By the late fourth and early third millennia B.C., the invention of pictographs and then cuneiform writing facilitated international links and trade between countries, spurring and spreading further developments in art, literature, science and religion across the known world.

Flock of sheep along the Tigris-Euphrates river valley.

Political Status

The nations and empires of Mesopotamia enjoyed considerable political status in the ancient world, a reality that was directly dependent on their location as a hub of land and sea routes from Europe and Africa into Asia and back again. Through the easily navigable Persian Gulf to the Indian Ocean and Far East; across the Zagros Mountains into Persia, Afghanistan and on to the Horse and Silk Road of China; up the Euphrates Valley then across to Anatolia and the Mediterranean and Aegean seas; or down the Levant to the Red Sea, the Arabian Peninsula, Egypt, East Africa and beyond—Mesopotamia was truly a hub between east and west.

Since Mesopotamia was located at one of the most important crossroads in the ancient Near East, it was a place through which material and spiritual culture flowed to and from neighboring countries. Here, peoples, and everything that defined their identities, mingled in a vast and intricate mosaic. Throughout ancient history, the region of Mesopotamia—in whole or in part—was ruled by peoples that entered from the four corners of the ancient Near East: Elamites, Medians and Persians from the east; Sumerians, Chaldeans and Semites from the south; Kassites, Assyrians and Hittites from the north; Amorites and Greeks from the west, and others. The major problem facing the various rulers of Mesopotamia was twofold: unification and control of its interior regions on the one hand, while on the other keeping the next invader at bay. In fact, very few kingdoms were successful in doing so for long.

THE MEDITERRANEAN BASIN

Introduction

The lands of the ancient Near East were strung along the Fertile Crescent, balanced on either end by two thin river valleys and squeezed by the climactic uncertainties of the deserts and mountains that encroached along their entire length. In sharp contrast, the Mediterranean world can be seen as a vast amphitheater in which the sea draws the lands along its shore together, while an almost unbroken outer circle of mountains and deserts served to keep the enemies beyond at bay. These two worlds, east and west, are nevertheless tied together through geography, and from the earliest days their respective peoples were drawn to interact with each other for commercial and military interests.

It is only natural that a body of water as large and dominant as the Mediterranean would have been called by many names in the ancient world. For the Assyrians and Babylonians, this was the "Upper Sea" because of its location beyond the upper Euphrates River. The Old Testament speaks of the "Western Sea" (Deut 11:24; Joel 2:20) lying on the western horizon of Israel, a horizon which seemed to stretch toward infinity. Phoenicians and others (Num 34:6–7 *et passim*) called the Mediterranean the "Great Sea" as it was far larger than any other known body of water. For the Greeks this was the "Inner Sea," bounded by lands that they knew, unlike the foreboding Atlantic Ocean, an unfamiliar "External" or "Outer Sea." The Romans introduced the word "Mediterraneum" ("middle land," i.e., a sea surrounded by various lands of importance to the Romans). The New Testament calls the Mediterranean simply "the Sea" (Acts 10:32, 27:30), while for the Talmud this was "Okiyanus," the Ocean (Tosefta, *Terumot* 82).

Geological Structure and Topography

The Mediterranean Sea is part of a much larger east-west topographical basin that includes the lowlands of the north Arabian Desert, the Tigris and Euphrates river valley and the Persian Gulf. To the north lies a great mass of mountains stretching from the Alps eastward through the Balkans and Anatolia to the Zagros, Caucasus and Elburz mountains above Mesopotamia and Iran, then eventually to the Himalayas in central Asia. This jumbled mass of snow-capped mountains exhibits features of complex folding and faulting, and has a long geological history. Above this are the plains and tablelands of central Europe and the interior of Russia, a different world altogether in which the geological relief is largely defined by wide-spaced river valleys. From here the greatest invasions into the Mediterranean world would eventually take place, including those of the Huns (5th century A.D.) and Turks (11th–16th centuries A.D.).

The Mediterranean Sea itself is circumscribed on the north and east by a number of relatively low mountain chains (those of Greece, Lycia and Pamphilia; the Taurus Mountains and

The climate and soil of the high central Anatolian Plateau, heartland of the Hittite Empire, is well suited for grazing and for grain.

In the early second millennium B.C. *the Assyrians established a trading center at Kanesh in this central Anatolian valley, and for over one hundred years controlled the historic route that ties Asia to Europe.*

the Lebanon Range). The coastline is largely concordant, that is, it tends to follow the direction of these lines of coastal mountains. This is the case for most of the Italian Peninsula, the western and eastern coasts of the Balkan Peninsula, southern Anatolia, and most of the Levant. In many places the coastal mountains drop directly into the sea, and even when they run at some distance from the coast the straight-line direction of the overall topography offers few major natural harbors. The coastal plains, however, are typically fertile for agriculture and offer a decent base for permanent human settlement. In contrast, the only areas of discordant coasts, where the mountain chains run at right angles to the Mediterranean, are southern Italy, the very southern end of the Balkans (the Peloponnesus), western Anatolia, and the northwestern corner of the Levant. Here large areas of protected water in deep inlets provided ample opportunity for seaborne communication to develop. It is not surprising that it was in the Aegean and from northern Phoenicia that Mediterranean sea trade thrived.

Various areas of human settlement, then, sprang up around the Mediterranean, either in connection with natural harbors or centered on fertile coastal plains. The coastal mountains tended to separate these regions from each other on land, hence further prompting sea travel. Among the more important coastal plains are those of Cilicia (ancient Kue) and Attalia (modern Antalya) on the southern Anatolian coast, the river deltas of the Meander and Hermus rivers in western Anatolia, the plain of Thessaly in eastern Greece, the Po river valley in northern Italy, and the plains along the western coast of Italy.

Anatolia is centered on a high plateau essentially isolated from the Mediterranean, Aegean and Black seas by rugged interior mountains. Here rainfall drains into the shallow, enclosed salt lake of Tuz Golu, with the great arc of the Halys River to the north circling to the Black Sea. This brutal landscape was the homeland of the Hittites, who used its natural defenses to launch an empire into the Levant in the late second millennium B.C. In the time of the New Testament this was the heartland of Galatia (Acts 16:6; Gal 1:2) and Cappadocia (Acts 2:1; 1 Pet 1:1). To the west, major drainage systems of Anatolia flowed into the Aegean, and here a gradual tapering in elevation provided numerous fertile agricultural valleys. This region, called Ionia by the Greeks but incorporated into the Roman Empire as Asia Minor, always maintained more suitable conditions for human settlement than the rest of Anatolia. Anatolia is separated from the Balkan Peninsula and Europe by a complicated depression forming the Bosphorus Strait (with an average width of only 1 mile), the Sea of Marmara and the Dardanelles (on average 3 miles [5 km] wide). Together these form one of most strategic and significant shipping channels on earth.

The Balkan Peninsula south of Mount Olympus (9,570 ft./2,920 m) was the heartland of ancient Greece, while to

These and many other "fairy chimney" formations of soft volcanic tuff were used as dwellings and monasteries from the ninth century A.D. on, in Cappadocia, central Anatolia.

the north lay the mountainous region of Macedonia. Due to prolonged and severe tectonic activity, the entire area of Greece is quite dissected and divided, and composed of an irregular series of mountain ranges all oriented more or less northwest-southeast, with many reaching elevations from 3,500 feet (1,100 m) to over 8,000 feet (2,400 m). Southern Greece, the Peloponnesus (properly Achaia in ancient Greek sources), a rough fig-leaf shaped landmass dangling into the Mediterranean by the narrow Isthmus at Corinth, is the most rugged of all both in terms of coastline and overall terrain in relation to size. Here no point inland is over 40 miles (65 km) from the sea. Altogether ancient Greece had an area of less than modern Portugal but a coastline longer than the entire Iberian or Italian peninsulas. The net result of the lay of the land in ancient Greece was twofold: (1) communities that sprang up in any of the numerous small intermountain valleys tended to be politically independent entities, while (2) the proximity to the sea prompted shared commercial and diplomatic interests.

Commercial interests centered on ports lining the western Anatolian and southeastern Greek coasts were pulled together by the islands of the Aegean Sea. Sailors in the Aegean are never out of sight of land until south of Crete, the largest of the Aegean islands, which is located in such a way so as to shelter the Aegean from the Mediterranean beyond. To the east is the island of Cyprus, from which the mountains of both Anatolia and Lebanon are visible, a line-of-sight which ensured that Cyprus would become a natural sea-bridge between the Mediterranean and the ancient Near East. For much of its history, then, Greece faced east, drawn by the islands and ports of the Aegean toward the eastern Mediterranean seaboard and beyond.

The boot-shaped Italian Peninsula slices deeply into the Mediterranean Sea, perfectly situated to dominate the east-west sea lanes that bind together the lands on the Mediterranean's perimeter. The straight-line backbone of the Italian Peninsula is formed by the Apennine Mountains that extend the full length of Italy. Although the Apennines rise to an average height of 4,000 feet (1,200 m), numerous mountain passes ensure that no area of settlement along the coastline is isolated from the others. Hence, the largely homogeneous character of the peninsula, in terms of geological structure but also climate, fertility and vegetation, served as a basis for political unification under Rome in the late first millennium B.C. In addition, the high wall of the Alps, rising dramatically from the fertile Po Valley in the north, provides an adequate defensive barrier for Italy's only land connection to the rest of the world. In spite of its lengthy coastline, Italy boasts few good natural harbors; the best in ancient times faced southwest. This fact, when combined with the reality that the best agricultural plains and hence largest cities (including Rome) were on the western coast, and the nearest islands—Corsica, Sardinia and Sicily—also lay to the west across the Tyrrhenian Sea, ensured that ancient Rome was first and foremost a western-oriented empire. With Greece facing east and Rome facing west, the Adriatic Sea dividing the Italian and Balkan peninsulas can be seen as an important east-west line in the Mediterranean.

Climate

The coastlands of the Mediterranean Basin largely share a similar climate, termed "Mediterranean," with cool, wet winters and hot, dry summers. Due to the prevailing rainfall, the western side of each region (western Italy, western Greece, western Anatolia, the western coast of the Levant) is wetter than its corresponding eastern side. Throughout, local variations in climate occur due to elevation and its effects on prevailing rainfall. In addition, annual rainfall amounts in any given region tend to vary dramatically, with a small margin any given year tipping the balance to feast or famine. The interior regions to the north are largely influenced by the climate of Europe. Hence, the cooler southern coast of the Black Sea (northern Anatolia) and upper Macedonia see precipitation throughout the year, with an autumn maximum and a spring minimum. This climate favors thick deciduous forests and heavy undergrowth, a rarity for the Mediterranean world. The high plateau of central Anatolia is arid and cold, with steppe grasslands suitable for grazing and grain. The climate of the western slopes of Anatolia is more moderate, allowing a wide variety of agricultural pursuits elsewhere limited by the heat of the Mediterranean summer and the dry winter cold of the Anatolian interior. It was in this favored region that some of the largest cities of Anatolia took root during the period of Roman dominance, and here the growth of the early church during and just after the time of the New Testament was pronounced. As for the Italian Peninsula, only the Po Valley in the north sees rain throughout the year, a fact that enhances its role as Italy's primary agricultural land.

Natural Resources and Routes

The primary natural recourses of the Mediterranean Sea, its agricultural fertility and mineral deposits, together with the network of land and sea routes tying the region together and linking it to lands beyond, provided the basic material for the commercial success of its various peoples.

Due to the mountainous character of Italy, Greece, Anatolia, Crete and Cyprus, only a fraction of these lands are arable, with mainland Greece (at 20%) and Crete (around 12%, and that mostly in rocky terraces) having the least amount of cultivable land. In Greece and Crete only a few

CULTURE AND COMMERCE IN THE ANCIENT NEAR EAST

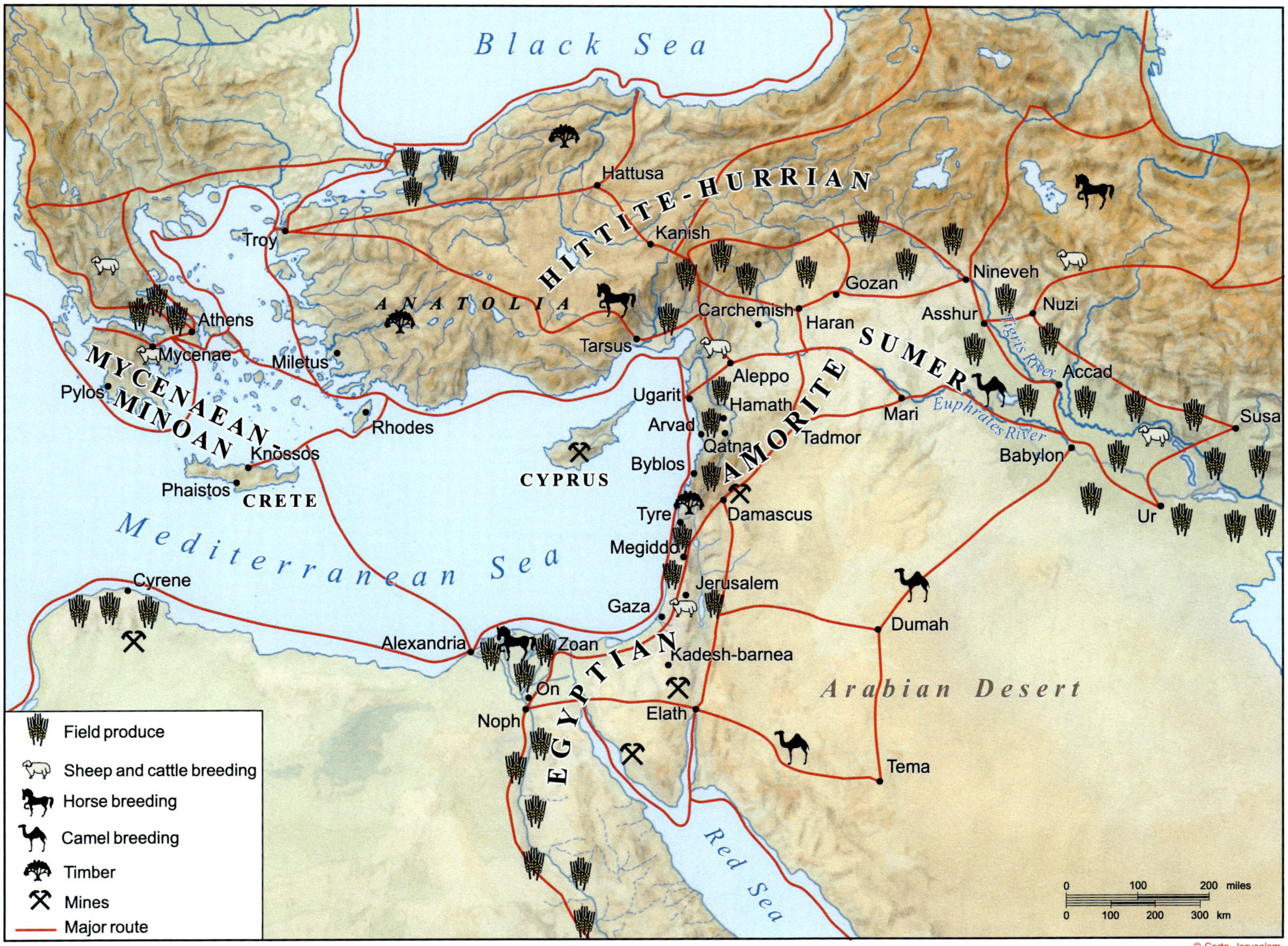

© Carta, Jerusalem

This small harbor at the site of Alexandria Troas (Acts 16:7–11) on the far western coast of Anatolia, with the Aegean island of Bozcaada off-shore, represents the network of sea routes that drew the lands of the Mediterranean together.

valleys are more than a dozen miles long and a few wide, although erosion has filled them with fertile alluvial soil. Throughout the Mediterranean a mixed economy prevailed: olives, vines and wheat in the warmer, lower valleys and plains; sheep, goats and pigs on the mid-range slopes; with grain (especially barley) and large cattle characterizing the cooler steppe lands. In addition, certain regions gained fame for specialized commodities, such as the plains of Thessaly in Greece and Cilicia (Kue) in Anatolia for war horses (cf. 1 Kgs 9:28). In antiquity many of the hills throughout the entire region were heavily forested, but already by the fifth century B.C. the effects of deforestation were felt in Greece as timber had to be imported from Macedonia and the southern Black Sea coast. The islands of Crete and Cyprus, their mountains largely denuded, have yet to recover their forests.

As for mineral deposits, silver mines near Athens helped to enrich the city as a center of learning and leisure, and from the earliest periods the silver, copper and iron deposits of Cyprus pulled that island into the trade network of the ancient Near East. Italy, too, had deposits of copper and iron, two commodities necessary for technological self-sufficiency in the ancient world. Marble can be found in Italy, Greece and Anatolia, with the green marble of eastern Greece most favored by the Roman emperors.

As for travel, the only river in the entire region that can truly be called navigable for any significant length was the Po, in the northern Italian Peninsula.

Greek merchant ship, 6th century B.C.

Others such as the Tiber, Meander and Hermus brought sea traffic inland to some extent, although the effects of silting over time tended to push their alluvial coastal plains out to sea; Ephesus, Miletus, Priene and Tarsus, all once port cities, are now inland as a result. Most watercourses, however, were narrow torrents, non-navigable in the winter because of the quick and violent flow of water and dry in the summer; during the summer, at least, their rocky beds could serve as local land routes. Among the strategic passes, none was more important than the Cilician Gates in southeastern Anatolia. Here, above Tarsus on the Cilician Plain, virtually all land traffic between Europe and Asia was funneled. In terrain as rugged as that which surrounds the Mediterranean, land routes were always difficult. Even after the advent of the Roman road system which greatly eased travel, a frequent traveler such as the Apostle Paul, a native of the great cosmopolitan center of Tarsus who traveled an estimated 15,000 miles (24,000 km) on his missionary journeys, would note:

> I have been on many journeys, in dangers from rivers, dangers from robbers . . . dangers in the city, dangers in the wilderness, dangers on the sea, dangers among false brethren. I have been in labor and hardship, through many sleepless nights, in hunger and thirst, often without food, in cold and exposure. (2 Cor 11:26–27)

Navigation on the Mediterranean Sea

In spite of the dangers inherent to long-distance sea travel, the economic advantages that sea routes held over land routes launched people into the Mediterranean:

1. A ship moves easily and inexpensively, borne for the most part by the power of the natural ocean currents (in the Mediterranean, these flow in a counterclockwise motion along the coasts) and by the winds that fill its sails.

2. Ships can carry cargoes hundreds of times heavier and bulkier than can be loaded on the backs of animals or in carts.

3. A sea passage needs no preparation or upkeep as does a road.

Long-distance seafaring voyages in the eastern Mediterranean usually followed a counterclockwise route: if starting from the Peloponnesus, a ship would sail to Crete, then be pushed by the prevailing winds to Egypt or the southern Levant (Israel), then hug the shores of the Levant, Cyprus and Anatolia to Rhodes and island-hop the Aegean back to Greece. The larger Mediterranean islands are located no more than 40 miles (65 km) from shore, a reasonable daily distance covered by a ship under sail, and the islands of the Aegean are within quick and easy sailing distance from each other. Voyages were usually undertaken in daylight, although eventually many inhabited islands had lighthouses to help guide sailors by night. Long voyages required many intermediary stops, not only to spend as many nights as possible under safe anchorage but also to engage in commerce at ports of trade and replenish the ship's provisions (Acts 21:1–8). Even the longest voyage without landfall typically taken by sailboat, that from Crete to Egypt, usually took only four to five days.

THE AEGEAN PEOPLES

The Aegean Peoples and Their Cultures

One cannot overestimate the vital role that the Mediterranean Sea has played throughout history for the peoples who have lived along its shores. Domination of sea routes was imperative, not only in the economic and social development of nations, but also in their political and military history. It is not surprising that history is replete with the struggles of various nations over the right to rule the shores and parts of the sea; among these are Minoans, Mycenaeans, various Sea Peoples, Phoenicians, Greeks and Romans.

The Minoan Culture. Crete is the largest island on the Aegean Sea. With a comfortable climate it served as the main crossroads for shipping between the eastern Mediterranean—where sailing was relatively easy—and the central Mediterranean around the Italian Peninsula. The island's greatest length is 155 miles (250 km), with a maximum width of some 35 miles (55 km). Crete's mountains rise to 8,038 feet (2,450 m) above sea level, and were forested in antiquity with cypress, pine, and perhaps even cedar trees. Crops such as grains, grapevines, and olives were cultivated in the island's few arable areas, and the inhabitants engaged in fishing. Thus, Crete's sailors and farmers could supply provisions to the foreign ships that came from all directions and anchored at the island.

The Cretans, whose origins were evidently in Asia Minor and Greece, established their capital at Knossos (modern Heraklion), on the island's northern tableland, opposite the Greek mainland, a location that was safest in times of storm. A second important center was Phaistos, on the southern

In the mid- to late second millennium B.C. *the Mycenaeans dominated the sea lanes of the eastern Mediterranean from their homeland in the hills and valleys of the eastern Peloponnesus, shown here.*

coast facing Egypt. Thus the Cretans provided a link between Greece, Egypt and the Levant, but also had connections to Italy and Spain. Their commercial and military significance, then, becomes obvious.

The Minoan culture (named after their legendary king, Minos) that developed in Crete established commercial and cultural ties to Mesopotamia and Egypt in the third millennium B.C. Minoan culture reached its peak in the sixteenth century B.C., and is attested archaeologically in Cyprus, Ugarit and the Levant, Mesopotamia, Egypt, the Italian Peninsula, Sicily and Sardinia.

The Mycenaean Culture. The Mycenaeans appear to have been descendants of Achaean tribes that penetrated southward into the Peloponnesus from northern Greece. They farmed along river estuaries and mountain slopes, and later developed manufacturing. Archaeology has revealed evidence of distinctive Mycenaean products: enormous clay vessels for storing oil and wine, copper utensils from ore imported from Cyprus, and articles of ivory that have been found in Megiddo. Important Mycenaean cities included Mycenae, Corinth, Tiryns, and Argos.

During its height in the fifteenth and fourteenth centuries B.C., Mycenae was a strong competitor of Crete in maritime trade; with the fall of Knossos and the other Cretan cities in 1400 B.C., the Mycenaeans inherited control of the

A Mycenaean funerary mask of thin gold, found in a Mycenaean shaft grave, 1550–1500 B.C.

(below) A Mycenaean IIIA2 kylix, from Acco.

THE ISLAND OF CRETE

THE MIGRATION OF THE SEA PEOPLES, 1174 B.C.

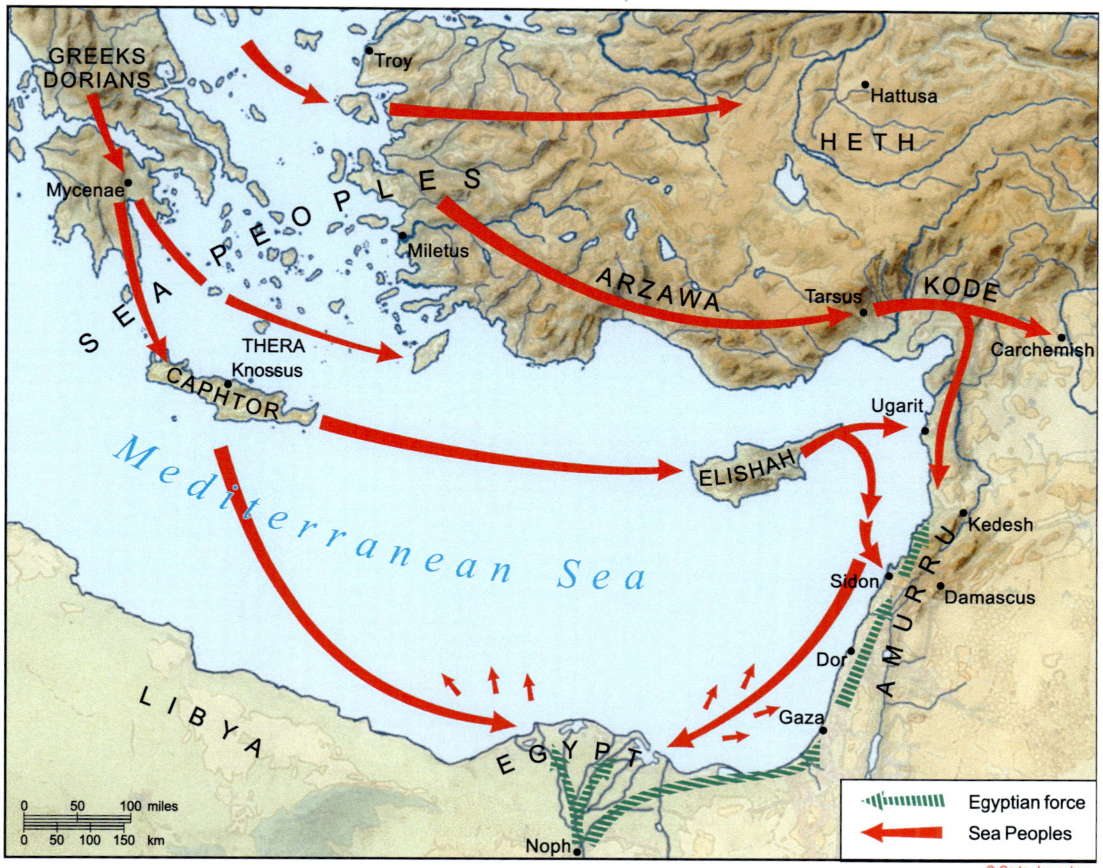

Prisoners from among the Sea Peoples, on relief of Rameses III (1195–1164 B.C.) at Medinet Habu, Egypt.

commerce of the eastern Mediterranean from Egypt to the Aegean. They controlled the islands of Rhodes and Cyprus and the port of Ugarit in the northern Levant, all of which served as settlements where the Mycenaeans traded with Mesopotamia and the Hittites. Mycenaean ships were constructed in the shipyards of Ugarit, and warehouses for importing and exporting goods were built in all the ports of the eastern Mediterranean. Mycenaean pottery, especially large storage vessels for oil and wine, has frequently been found in archaeological digs throughout the eastern Mediterranean, including many in Canaan/Israel: Jaffa, Ashkelon, Gaza, Lachish, Beth-shemesh, Gezer, Jerusalem, Shechem, Taanach, Megiddo, Hazor, Beth-shean, and Jericho. These and other sites provide a "map" of Mycenaean commercial interests in the eastern Mediterranean. Mycenae was destroyed with the Dorian invasion from northern Greece in the twelfth century B.C.

The Sea Peoples. By the end of the thirteenth century B.C., the established power centers in the eastern Mediterranean began to break apart. While many factors surely contributed to this widespread decline in organized social and political structures, one that tends to be emphasized by all historians of the period is the movement of peoples from the region of the Aegean to the east and southeast. Who these people were, where they originated and why they left their homeland(s) are all debated. No doubt this was a prolonged process by many different groups for a variety of reasons. In any case, Egyptian sources of the mid-twelfth century B.C. speak of invasions into the Nile Delta and along the southern coast of the Levant by peoples from the sea, hence the modern phrase "the invasion of the Sea Peoples" to label the entire phenomenon. Among the groups that ended up settling on the southern Levantine coast were the Philistines, whose original homeland, according to the prophet Amos, was Caphtor (=Crete; Amos 9:7). Other groups such as the Sherden and Tjekker apparently settled on the coast farther north. The Philistines, from whom the later geographical term "Palestine" is derived, established a loose confederation of city-states between Gaza and Ekron at the same time that Israel was settling the hill country to the east; their skirmishes over the region's limited resources is well attested in the Bible (Judg 13–16; 1 Sam 4–17).

The Phoenicians. The rise of the Phoenicians led to two historic changes in the eastern Mediterranean. For the first time in the history of the region, a Semitic people controlled the sea routes of the Mediterranean, and for the first time a people tiny in land area and population became a major maritime power, sailing not only the Mediterranean but the Red Sea (1 Kgs 9:26–28) and part of the Indian Ocean as well.

The name "Phoenicia" evidently derives from *phoinike*, a Greek word meaning "purple-red." Apparently the Phoenicians were among the first to perfect the technique of extracting and producing a rare and valuable purple-red dye from sea snails found on the northern Levantine coast. This dye was used to color fine-quality linen, wool, and silk cloth, and became a symbol for royalty.

Phoenicia was located along the narrow eastern coastlines of what are now Syria, Lebanon, and northern Israel, altogether nearly 300 miles (480 km) in length. Phoenician

The Economy of the Kingdom of Tyre, According to Ezekiel 27

Local Products

Natural Resources	*Manufactured Products*
Cypress from Senir	Lumber for building ships
Cedars of Lebanon	Masts for ships
Shipyards in Gebal	Shipbuilding
Purple and blue dyes	Dyed cloth, embroidered clothing
Ships and sailors from Tarshish	Ships for transporting metals
Fish	Fresh and salted fish

Cedars of Lebanon

Imports

Product	*Origin*	*Manufactured Product and Commercial Use*
Bashan oak	Bashan, in land of Israel	Masts for ships
Woven linen cloth	Egypt	Ship sails
Blue, purple dyes	Cyprus (Elishah)	Dyed sails
Metals	Spain	Silver, iron, tin, lead utensils
Copper	Asia Minor	Copper and brass utensils
Human beings	Asia Minor	Slave trade
Horses, mules	Togarmah—Anatolia	Pulling carriages
Ivory, ebony	Dedan in Arabia, East Africa	Art objects, statues
Woven cloth	Egypt	Clothing, rope, sails
Gemstones	Arabia	Jewelry
Grain, honey, balm, oil	Land of Israel	Food, cosmetics, offerings
Wine, wool	Damascus	Food, dyed woven cloth
Rugs, saddlecloths	Dedan in Arabia	Household use, riding
Lambs, goats	Arabia, Kedar	Woven wool clothing, dyed raw wool
Spices, precious stones, gold	Kingdom of Sheba	Cosmetics, jewelry

port cities at home included Arvad, Gebal (Byblos), Sidon and Tyre. The Phoenicians also established international ports at Cyprus, Rhodes, the Aegean Islands, Crete, Sicily, Malta, Sardinia, Utica, Carthage, and Cadiz in Gibraltar.

Limestone relief depicting the head of a Phoenician nobleman, from Dor.

Phoenician merchant ship, 7th century B.C.

With the high Lebanon Mountains protecting its back and a jagged, harbor-friendly coastline at its feet, Phoenicia faced the sea and developed a thriving trade economy that, by the mid-first millennium B.C. reached the western Mediterranean. Thus, Ezekiel called the Kingdom of Tyre "the merchant of the peoples" (Ezek 27:3) in a discourse that clearly recognized Phoenicia's role as a middleman for international trade in both practical and exotic goods (Ezek 27:12–25). Chief among trade products imported by the Phoenicians were basic foodstuffs grown in the land of Israel (Ezek 27:17; Acts 12:20), for Phoenicia didn't have enough agricultural land to support itself. Phoenicia's chief home-grown export was lumber (primarily cedar and cypress) cut from the Lebanon Mountains; biblical writers praised the strength of these forests (2 Kgs 19:23; Isa 14:8, 60:13) and both Solomon and the Egyptian pharaohs imported lumber for royal building projects (1 Kgs 5:7–10).

The political, economic, and maritime status of the Phoenicians required superior abilities of organization, planning, and administration. The inhabitants of Tyre in particular earned renown as skilled sailors who lived facing the Mediterranean at the "entrance to the sea"; their border was "in the heart of the seas" (Ezek 27:3–4). Tyrians were known to be adroit merchants with vision (Isa 23:8), brave and daring men of war (Ezek 27:10–11), and superb and resourceful craftsmen and artisans with great initiative (Ezek 27:16, 28:13).

Rabbi Shimon ben Lakish testified to the wealth of Tyre and its kingdom, to the abundance of its products and to the ease of life for its inhabitants when he said, "There is no 'land of the living' (Ps 116:9) but Tyre and its hinterland, and Cyprus and its hinterland, where things are inexpensive and there is plenty"(*Gen Rabbah* 74:1; J.T. *Kela'im* 9:4).

The strategic importance of the Dardanelles cannot be overestimated. Not only does this narrow channel separate Greece and Europe from Anatolia and Asia, it also provides the only sea route between the Mediterranean and Black seas.

Greek City-states and the Spread of Hellenism. From the fall of the Mycenaean civilization around 1200 B.C. to the mid-eighth century B.C., Greece fell into a so-called "Dark Age" and was a minor player in the Aegean, while being nearly invisible on the larger world stage. It was during this time, however, that Greece absorbed and adapted important cultural traits from the ancient Near East, including the alphabet (from Phoenicia) and religious motifs that would form the basis of later classical Greek and Roman mythology. Seeds were sown for a pan-Hellenism that began to flower with the rise of independent, rival city-states during the Archaic Age (c. 750–500 B.C.); chief among these were Corinth, Athens and Sparta. This period saw the beginning of colonization throughout the Aegean and Ionia (western Anatolia), and in Cyrene in North Africa. The Classical Age (c. 500 B.C. to the rise of Alexander in 334 B.C.) was characterized not only by great cultural achievements in political science, literature, philosophy and the arts, but also by a resurgence of Greek commercial and military interests throughout the eastern Mediterranean. This "Triumph of Greece" was checked somewhat by a series of wars with the Persians on Greek soil in the early fifth century B.C. Alexander's push to the Indus Valley (334–323 B.C.) and the subsequent efforts to colonize various parts of the land that he had conquered spread the cultural grip of Hellenism throughout the rest of the eastern Mediterranean and the ancient Near East, while the wealth of the world flowed to the Aegean. The pendulum of commercial and cultural influence had swung to the West, where it was to remain for centuries.

Of particular relevance for the world of the Bible, many Jews followed the wake of these new social and economic opportunities into the lands of the Mediterranean; the result was a vibrant Jewish Diaspora that, among other things, provided avenues of contact for the emergent Church in the first and second centuries A.D. This contact with Hellenism also posed serious religious and social challenges to the Jews of Galilee, Judea and especially Jerusalem in their struggle to remain faithful to the "traditions of the ancestors" while becoming relevant to a changing world.

(left) Heinrich Schliemann dug this massive cut into the ruins of Troy in the 1870s, prompting a historic reassessment of the great Trojan War described by Homer in the Iliad. *The Plain of Troy, ancient Greece's foothold in Anatolia, and the Aegean lie beyond.*

(below) This white marble Temple of Trajan in Pergamum in western Anatolia represents Rome's economic, cultural and military hold on the Mediterranean world by the early second century A.D. *For better or worse, the roads connecting the widely diverse geographical regions of the known world now all led to Rome.*

Rome and the Legacy of the Mediterranean World

The relative latecomers, but eventual champions, in the entire ancient history of the Mediterranean were the Romans. The traditional founding of Rome dates only to 753 B.C., and while early attempts by Etruscans to create a viable urban fabric in the mid-Italian Peninsula were relatively successful, their efforts to unify the land politically were not. The Republic, centered on Rome, did gain political control over Italy during a long and difficult struggle in the fifth and fourth centuries B.C., and managed to secure their borders to the north (Gaul) and west. The third century B.C. saw a series of wars with Greece and Greek colonies such as Carthage, as Rome now had the resources and incentive to begin to forge an eastern empire. By the time of the New Testament, Rome had established control along the eastern Mediterranean seaboard, and by the early second century A.D. had taken the Arabian spice trade from the Nabateans and was able to exert a degree of control over the Parthians in Mesopotamia. From Britain and Spain to Egypt and Mesopotamia, Rome reigned supreme. While this new political reality carried some benefit for everyone—with *pax Romana* came economic opportunities, a relative ease of travel and the headiness of being a citizen of the world—there were clear drawbacks: the economic resources of far-flung lands such as Judea were bled for Rome's benefit, and peoples who preferred their own ancestral traditions over those of their conquerors were faced with difficult choices regarding loyalty and identity. The survival of Judaism and the spread of Christianity in the Roman world are testimonies to mankind's abilities both to adapt and to hold firm in the face of change in lands in which historical and cultural roots run deep.